You Are God

MARY

DeVORSS & COMPANY
P.O. Box 550
Marina Del Rey, California 90294-0550

Twelfth Printing, 1987

ISBN: 0-87516-057-3

Printed in the United States of America

DEDICATION

Each one who reads this book becomes owner of at least a part of it. To him or her, then, are dedicated the eternal truths within these pages.

FOREWORD

I have little desire to insert the personal pronoun into this book, but a short explanation seems necessary so you may understand that I, Mary, am no more than a secretary for the lessons following. I was under direction at all times while working on the beautiful words which came into my mind as I sat with my fingers on the keys of my typewriter.

Some unseen mind dictated one complete lesson to me telepathically each time I felt an urge to write. There were several individuals involved in the series of twenty lessons, each distinct personalities to me. They possessed individual styles of phrasing and varying degrees of power in putting their thoughts across the spaces into my mind.

The two personal messages included in the lessons were not omitted, but only because I feel I have no right to delete or add to the works of others.

I can accept no plaudits for whatever benefit this book offers to a humanity seeking the truths of its universe in almost frantic, fearful search. Also I cannot take upon myself any censure, any criticism for words which may offend certain sensitive individuals. Many of the ideas or thoughts presented were entirely new to me, and some were completely contradictory to my own convictions.

Like one who reads this for the first time, You Are God is a source of surprise, amazement, knowledge and comfort to me after many readings, and doubtless with each new one I shall find new food for thought.

Readers usually feel some curiosity about an author as a rule, but that is precisely what I do not intend satisfying. In myself I am nothing except that which God has let me be and that which I have made of my surface self in this lifetime. I will receive the title credit for this book, but I did not change one word of those which came to me from outside myself. The true authors are anonymous and prefer to remain that way. Likewise I prefer the shadows of anonymity.

It might be well to mention the strange language

of one paragraph in the last lesson. I cannot offer any other explanation than that given to me — that it is an ancient language used by the wise ones, and in this particular instance is a chant of blessing.

You will notice that all reference to God as "he" or "him" is not capitalized. It was so dictated to me and so it remains. I find that in reading of our Lord as "he" and "him" I have reached a new closeness to him, a warm intimacy completely erasing the old, awe-struck attitude I once possessed toward my creator. There is no insolence intended, no lack of reverence. The Lord is my entire being and all the world is in him also.

By this creed I attempt to live as a normal human being, by this creed I search for personal improvement, by this creed I hope to die in the right time.

I am Mary, who says to you that the only way to God is your own, not the leading of another or the pushing of another. If the lessons in this book are a guidance to your feet or an inspiration to seek your own way, then I have not lived this lifetime in vain, or spent the moments with my beloved brothers for no purpose.

May you go with God always, in his ways and in his light. There can be no life without him and there is no death with him.

Chapter I

This is the beginning, that all things be told in their proper order as all things of God's world and universe are in their proper order. First the dawn of day, then the sun's full glowing, the quiet time of preparation for the journey of the sun into the sea, the soft fall of night, the blanket of the world, the full darkness in which all things of creation come to realization of the vast spaces of timelessness, asleep or awake.

Herein lies the secret knowledge of how best to live the life of a physical being during the season known to man as an existence. With the dawn, come into the active realization of your practical affairs and duties. Make them pleasurable to you as the known plans for your present lifetime, and fulfill them with your heart as well as your hands.

In the heat of the heart of the sun, pause for the refreshment your soul will be in need of, for the pull from your source of energetic supply will have depleted it enough to call upon the channel of power to replace that which you have given. During the lull which falls before the sun has been removed from your sight in order to shine on all in the circle of God, feel the peace begin to descend about you and so let it be absorbed within you.

Night truly brings the full beauty and serenity of creation for the knowing to experience and be renewed through. Space is the great existence of the universe within which you are at present living. The stars are the lights by which the angels of the heavens show their wings to the seekers whose vision can travel far enough to cross the shallows and rapids of earth-atmosphere and encompass the greatness of the simple truth.

Your cup truly runs over with the waters of the joys to be found in walking straight and truly the path toward knowledge as it is presented to you.

You reach a point of fulfillment within your being that pulls you toward the star of your destiny. Each of God's creations has a star of his own, and thus the heavens are filled with count-less star-lights by which to guide the way of the night-traveler, that he may not be lost as he seeks his own.

It is true that many crossroads are met and many wrong ways taken, but alternate roads are always planned in advance to take care of unexpected detours and washouts. The paths left open to you are as good and as fated for your full happiness as any you have missed or ignored. There is always the highest hope and the deepest joy in the meeting of your intended pattern, though it be later than originally planned, even unto the last moments of physical life.

Secret seem the ways of God's planned existence because the loss of knowledge among most men took place long ago, when the world of the planet Earth was a more perfect and more advanced thing than it is now or has been since. Only in the hearts of the truly humble and of the workers sent from the heavens has the truth lived on, to be dispensed as widely as possible while still shielding it from the scoffing and unbelieving that they might not dirty it with their soiled words.

Many times the civilizations of the Earth planet would have gone on to great spiritual understanding and greater material attainment than any can imagine if only greed and avarice had given way to the love and sacrificial spirit that live within all.

God has given each a small part of himself, that in the quiet moments of prayer the being's words can reach him and be known unto him so he may answer those prayers which are sincerely asked and rightly to be fulfilled. There is no need to shout aloud, for he quietly waits within to be recognized and summoned. There is no need to bow the head or bend the knee, for he calls on no man for obeisance, only for awareness.

No one has the right to tell another how to worship or how to live. That right is the one which makes all who are born free and equal, and it is given by God to all who have the priceless gift of his creation. There are many colors, sizes, types of beings which breathe the air of the physical world, but there is only one God and therefore only one kind of soul, or inner being, in each and every one.

God created in his own image the eternal selves within. Remember this when a black man who is lame stands beside a white, in need of help to cross the street. Remember this when a Jew stands beside a Catholic, in need of a drink of water and helpless to serve himself because his hands are twisted with arthritis. Remember this when a Chinese stands beside a Mexican, and looks at him with the eyes of sorrow which he cannot outwardly express.

There is no barrier to language anywhere in God's universe. All men have eyes in which to write their soul-messages, and that is all anyone needs to live in contentment with his neighbor or to travel in peace among the unknown places of the world. Look into your companion's eyes and let him look deep within yours.

For those whose physical eyes are blinded let this be a reminder: When heart speaks to heart, what need is there for lips to move and bring forth sound, or for eyes to know the light of material day?

To live by the Golden Rule is to put into action one of the basic precepts upon which the universe was founded, for love is the greatest unit of power created by God for the use of man, and the fullest answer to any cry for help. No one has ever found the boundaries of the heart, and its capacity has never been known to be less than endless.

Make all of your life the expression of your worship to God, and your awareness of the beauty with which he has surrounded you. He created the physical world to be one of loveliness and happiness. That man has made it full of the sorrows and dangers with which it is infested today is one of the greatest examples of how wrong the material being can be in action.

Set your goal far beyond that which an unknowing one could accomplish, for by affirming your faith and living it you will prove in the name of God that these things you believe do exist and are all-powerful. In the example of the true believer lies the convincing truth which will once again provide the light to show the way to those who have been lost in the darkness of ignorance and misunderstanding.

Chapter II

Will is the mind at its most powerful. The spiritual being cannot be overcome by the will at any time, thus proving that material self is subservient to spiritual self when the inner being is allowed full control.

Many moons ago, when the world lay in the stillness of spiritual embryo, God planned its destiny. He took the heart of his own servants and fastened it with unbreakable cord to the heart of man.

He took the great current of power which ran throughout his universe and connected it by invisible silver wires to the awareness of man.

He took the seas and the mountains of his own eternal kingdom and presented them for the seeking within the mind of man. They still represent the mysterious depths beyond mortal knowing of the wonders within man's world, and the heights beyond any physical attainment of the mysterious spaces surrounding the earth, into which only the mountains can maintain an unchanging contact.

Awareness is the key to further awareness and so to greater understanding and knowledge.

To be aware of the trees about is to be made aware of their actual living, breathing existence. To realize even the trees have selves brings forth the understanding of the life which inhabits all material things of this earth. This in turn provokes the thought processes into a knowledge that here indeed is proof of all things coming from the same God-source.

As in the proven existence of the same basic materials for creation of all matter, so lies truth in the existence of one basic belief by which man draws inner sustenance.

In other languages, with different words, each religion offers the same great and simple fact — that true faith in a man's heart leads him in the right direction regardless of his mode of travel. Whether he kneels before an idol, a priest or an altar of his own making, it is his complete trust which carries him to heights beyond his material world.

God created many colors, that all men should

not be alike in their enjoyment of beauty.

He created many climates, that all men should not be alike in their physical attributes.

Likewise has he sent many great ones to teach truths in many ways, for each man is what he is individually and must follow his own choosing.

Some who would travel from one place to another would go by train. Others would drive that they might be masters of their own mode of transportation. Some would prefer an airplane, for the destination would be their greatest aim. But still others would choose an ox-cart, knowing their goal waited for them always, and preferring to move slowly that they might savor every small and big experience along the way.

To each must be given his own path, his own way of traveling over it.

Those who run stumble oftener than those who walk, and those who fly have not the understanding which lies between two milestones, as would those who crossed by ox-cart.

God in his wisdom has made no mistakes. How then can any criticize his plans or his actions?

It is not for him to adjust his creation to the whims and desires of man, but rather for man to adjust his whims and desires to God's creation.

In this lies the full realization of true happiness for everyone who treads the earth.

Chapter III

Feel the force of God throughout your being whenever you give thought to the mighty wonders about you, not in rare moments of pleasure that you are among the beauties of his world, but often during every day and night. Give him thanks to make your own person more aware of these blessings each time, for in the expression of gratitude to God you will find yourself.

Make the most of each opportunity to savor the blessings he has heaped upon you and all your fellow beings. Breathe the incense of the flowers and know man has never created their like in all his years of experimenting with perfumes. Feel the hallowed quiet in the heights of the tallest mountains and know man has never duplicated the stillness in all his years of building churches in which to worship that which he brings to church within himself. See the colors of the physical world and know man has never painted their like in his greatest masterpieces, for there are no words with which to describe perfection and no pigments with which to picture it.

God has given the most beautiful things in his universe for all to enjoy free of charge. The serenity of sunset, the eternal aloofness of clouds, the soft carpet of the grass, the warmth of sunshine, the deep spaces of night, all are free. There is no charge for breathing the air of earth's atmosphere. There is no charge for running your fingers through the clean dirt which produces growing things. There is no charge for counting the stars at night or the seawaves by day. Nothing really worthwhile in living is bought with the coin of mortal man. Not one experience or possession can be secured with money.

The payment in God's universe is of far greater significance to man's eternal self than the coins of your world. There are no charge accounts in his kingdom, and all things are paid for by planned exchange, except that which a man would willfully take for himself before he has earned it or without right to it.

The balance wheel is never moved from its perfect position by God or his disciples, and if a man swings it from its mooring it rights itself at once, that the universe may remain in perfect balance. All things contribute to that state of being, small and large. The purest act of love and the basest act of hate shake the delicate balance so quickly another act must steady the wheel. Acts of love are compensated by other love and hate draws hatred, as surely as day draws the night.

Thus hangs all of the creation of God's making, all of his worlds without end. A man pays for what he wants most, for what he does, with the coin of his own choosing, of like mint. Does he choose to bestow upon his fellow man the best within his deepest self, paid in return he is with the richness of *better* self than before, and with a further knowledge of the rewards which range his roadside as he travels. Does he choose to inflict his will or his cruelty upon another, paid in return he is in the terrible responsibility of playing God with a human life, and the corrosion within his own soul of acid-like self-hatred.

Make the most of every day you live, for while each day often seems to have too many hours, the years have a knack for slipping by with such speed they are not missed until they have gone beyond recall or redemption. Life span in itself is so short as to be less than a moment in the history of eternity, but in the course of physical existence, a man must play the game of doing his best *now,* since there will be no re-playing of his record and no chance to undo that which has been done.

Live according to your own conscience. Not by what you think you should do or by what you think you should be, but by what you are. Not by the standards and codes of your neighbors or your business associates, but by those of your own heart. Not by the social practices of your circle of friends, but by the inner self which shines from within and acts only in love and kindness.

Hear this in the sincere humiliation of your true being and not with the ego of the material one: You are all things by yourself, for within lies the full strength of God, possessed by all to no greater or lesser degree than your own.

You are less than nothing without the force of God's great current running through you always, to sustain you in adversity and contain you in triumph.

You are the complete product of the might of God's ability as much as any being who walks the earth, and your worth is as great as the greatest, as small as the least.

You have all you require for success, for recognition, for fulfillment in your material atmosphere, for you possess that before which nothing can remain immovable — the touch of God.

You have always had and always will have the inner serenity, the pure love, and the irresistible power to accomplish your spiritual tasks, your daily duties and your heart's desires.

Give full attention to nothing else and to no one else who would deter you from the full happiness which you can attain in this lifetime, and to which you are entitled.

There is no man who can say, "God has forsaken me," for he would then have to be forsaken by himself. This he cannot be. In the depths of human misery will be found a thick crust of materialism covering and hiding the spirit within, hampering its efforts to find the light of truth, shielding it from accomplishment of self-understanding and self-acceptance.

Learn to accept and respect yourself. You are

a human being, a product of God, as are all your fellowmen. You are no less and no more than they. Accept that you are not physically perfect and perhaps not all you would wish to be in the ways of the material world. Then learn to respect that fire which burns within and cannot be quenched in its thirst to be made known. Respect the true you who carries you across the deserts of sorrow, the seas of despair, and leaves you tired but surviving on the far shores.

Pride is a product of material man. It is false and misleading and causes only misery to follow in its wake. Too often, however, is pride confused with the true human value of dignity. You must learn to conquer and remove pride from your mind completely if you would find the higher paths of the truth, but likewise you must make dignity an integral part of your being. It is the untouchable part of you which holds others at their proper distance when they would lay hands upon you in unwanted closeness or make their minds a part of yours. It is the unassailable part of you which cannot be destroyed by physical indignity or soiled by the surroundings of your present life.

Know then the difference between the two,

that you may become strong in the one as you become humble in the other. There is no degradation in accepting a sincere apology, and certainly none in giving one. There is no surrender in the voicing of good thoughts before another has had his turn. There is no sorrow in facing truth and voicing that discovery.

Make your life what it should be by the warmest, most sincere actions wherever you go, whatever you do. Make your happiness what it should be by expressing truly that which is within, regardless of outer surroundings. Make your self what it should be by conquering the egotistical surface self and showing the light of the inner being to all of your world.

This is the truth of the existence planned for man by the great God in the beginning of his creation. Win victory over your mortal self and you win victory over all your world, for *you* are everyone and everyone is *you*. Put your trust in God's keeping and he will put his work in your hands. There is no greater glory, no other goal, not any further reason for existing.

Make your working motto — The Lord is my shepherd. I shall not want.

Chapter IV

In your heart of hearts is the worship for only the true and the mighty presence of God. Less than that would find no place in the central core of your being, for you are the sum of perfect love and understanding which defines the mighty God as well as any phrase of mortal man.

There are no descriptions for him in the physical world. Man has tried for many centuries to find God and present a concrete definition of his self to the rest of the world, but it is an impossible task. Even the master ones cannot define him for you.

He can only be realized in the presence within you of serenity and happiness, in the atmosphere about you of beauty and life, in the spaces beyond you of his power and awesome size. Realize God and you will seek no definition of him, no answers to why, when and where, no explanation of your station or your pathway in life. Believe and you will know. Trust and you will understand. Love and you will grow. Give and you will be served.

Bit by bit is a small puzzle made whole, or a great building raised from the dust of the ground. So bit by bit must be built the structure of your understanding and of your ability to make that understanding active. Only the mighty ones whom God has seen fit to send to this planet employ his laws in their fullest intent, and even they sometimes slip into the ways of human beings as they live in the guise of mortals. To these goes then the double task of regaining the understanding they have lost and fulfilling their appointed work of showing the light of God's highways to the seeking.

Before there can be dawn, there must be night. Before there can be birth, there must be conception. Before there can be accomplishment, there must be struggle. Before there can be a finish, there must be a beginning.

Seek the beginning of your pathway with serenity and full trust that it will be shown to you if you but search with faith and patience. Let not the experiences of others sway or discourage your personal search, for yours is like that of none other. All the words of all the books in the world will not carry you one step along your marked trail either unless they coincide with those words which are engraved on your heart. Those words say – My God is me. I am my God. I can leave my life in no better hands, my heart is no greater heart. I am afraid of nothing, I demand nothing, I force nothing.

Within the circle of those who know the truth and are eager to guide those who seek it, live beings whose sole purpose is to hold high their lights that you may see your steps. They do not tell you where next to place your foot, or which way to turn. They only desire to give you illumination for the finding of your own way.

Let this then be your guide when you are in doubt as to whether you gain wisdom from the mouth of another, or strength from the domination of another. The truly humble are the great ones, for they are seeing the might of God before their eyes in all its splendor and it almost blinds them with its blazing perfection. Before this they hide their faces and are exalted by the knowledge they are less than nothing in comparison to that which is our Lord.

Know then he who boasts of his psychic abilities

is limiting himself to the borders of the unseen world which lies about you and along which lurk the ignorant, the fearful, the mischievous and the malignant. Only beyond does the light break upon the true spiritual world and shed its radiance for all to absorb and spread among the eager of the mortal plane.

Argue not against another who says you are wrong and he is right. If a man believes with his whole heart, though it be directly opposed to your own convictions, then he is not wrong. If your whole heart is open to your beliefs, then you are not wrong also. How then can you argue, for neither can lose.

If an individual is in need of your help it will be made known to you that he seeks guidance, and you must then give him not only the best which lies within you, but all of the best. It will be renewed twice and thrice over, and as he gains so do you grow. There is never any waste in God's kingdom, and especially how this is true of the inner seeking of man for God himself!

Heart to heart stand you with all you encounter. Overlook physical unattractiveness. Understand material aggressiveness. Give only awareness to the spirit shining from within, no matter how deep, how well covered. In your look of love and your act of friendship you will slough off some of the crust of self-deceit and the armor of fear worn by even the most antagonistic.

Deep in the center of the being exists an unerring recognition of God's power in action. There are times when you look into the eyes of another human being and are lost in the depths of their mystery. This is because your self knows that being's power for what it is, but your surface has been allowed to rule for too long and too blindly. It cannot see that which it is looking at directly.

Learn to understand the invisible pull exerted by certain ones in your path of life. Above all, do not mistake the animal-like magnetism exuded by those steeped in animalism. Know the true drawing by its irresistible feeling and by the mystery about the individual sending forth the vibrations. There is an arresting, unknown current too strong to be ignored by the most ignorant, opposed by the most unbelieving.

Grieve not if you have not yet achieved the heights of understanding which lead to true happiness and acceptance of all life offers. There is always time in which to find your way, and in the finding remember, no matter how seemingly long the search, you have acquired much valuable understanding and absorbed many valuable lessons.

When man understands his fellow man there will be no more wars, no more lies, no further crime, no illness, no misery. When the rules of the land are those of God and not politicians, there will be no need for prisons, policemen, hospitals, charity organizations.

This time will come upon the earth though it seems eons away at present, for in perfection was the earth created and perfection it will attain before the span of its use is done.

Other places have achieved or continued this state of being, and they are worlds of beauty and happiness such as mortal earth-beings have but dreamed over. There is no sickness, no crime; there is no poverty, no want; there is no fear, no ignorance. There are no wild animals and no wild people. Government is by a body of beings who truly rule by the will of all, for all are in accord. The great resources placed by God for practical use are employed in their true intent

—atomic power to fuel transportation, chemicals with which to treat metals for machinery, animals to become friends to, that the full creation of God—man—may better understand his potentials. Beings are alive only to fulfill their daily tasks, to help one another, and to give love to all specifically and generally.

This then can be the state of earth's being, when men stop closing the fist and begin opening the palm toward the gift of understanding. When they stop closing the ears and begin opening the heart to the fact that all are one to God, any color, any creed. When they stop running in fear and begin walking toward the light that waits in full view on the top of every hill.

It lies within the most obscure bootblack and the most prominent official to contribute toward earth's perfection, for none can defect if the balance *is* to be perfect. Someone must begin somewhere.

Why not you? Why not all within the scope of these words? Why not all those who can be reached by the example of active faith and understanding? A small beginning is life itself, but it ends in a burst of Glory such as is unknown to any other experience. So shall you work, a small unit in the vast whole of existence, but a beginning toward the ultimate goal of the successful conclusion of God's great experiment, for that is what we are, the seen and the unseen, the great and the small.

Know this in your heart of hearts, that the time may be shortened when you can once again be a true part of the flow of God's consciousness for eternity.

Chapter V

Wisdom is the key to riches far beyond the dreams of mortal man. Words are lost in the vast spaces of timelessness when the true source of all knowledge has been touched. Words are inadequate, unnecessary. They are but physical instruments by which physical thoughts are made known between physical beings. Words have the power to destroy, to create; to repulse, to attract; to express all emotion on the mortal plane. But they cannot say the feeling of soaring into the atmosphere of the planes beyond, or the knowing of the presence of God within one, or the exaltation of love from heart to heart in the ever-existing world.

Give heed to these matters that you do not mistake the golden tongue of a physical one for the golden heart of a true being. Remember the inadequacy of any vocabulary for description of the real and the deep that you do not overlook the quiet one in the background who seemingly is overshadowed by the loquacious one who holds the attention of the multitude with his oratory. Beware of the hole at your feet yawning deep and dark for your next step when your ears listen to the false music of the siren-song which would lure you to destruction. It is as nothing beside the true music sung in the universal chorus of praise to God, sung not in words but in melody, harmony, rhythm, and high-beating hearts pulsating in unison.

God in his wisdom made known to man the knowledge of his existence and his eternal presence. He made known to man the reality of the heartbeat which welds all hearts into one, the current of the universe which connects all awarenesses. But he left it to man to discover for himself the material ways of living, the devious paths by which to cheat, lie or steal from a fellow being, the greed, the selfishness, the self-centeredness of determination.

Wise is he who knows it is God's will which is the right will to obey, not his own. Blessed is he who knows it is his destined path which is the right direction in which to travel, not the turnings of his desires or whims. Won has he who knows his life is but an expression of God, to be expressed by his works, the tasks he accomplishes, not by his money or other wordly possessions.

The name of the Lord is the name of all creation. Therefore, all of creation is the Lord. You are God, the skies are God, the earth itself is God. Lesser in magnitude, lesser in expression, but as magnificent, each in its smaller way, as our Lord himself.

Strong are they with the current who feel within the radiant happiness of awareness. Forward goes the step of him who knows he is at all times an active part of God's plan, though he till the soil or simply read a book. Benign is the light upon him who looks toward the light, who worships the God he feels pulsing within himself, who knows the truth of the mighty waves of realization should physical life cease and the eternal life continue unhampered.

Believe, believe in the spaces of eternity, that your happiness will come to you and you may pass your days in fullness and richness. Let the windows of your soul be open to the light of God, and all things will come to you of the right.

Meet you any adversity of the physical world

and conquer it — nay, disintegrate it with the power of inner understanding which can encompass the universe within seconds and produce miracles instantaneously within the atmosphere about you. Be you, and you are fulfilled to the utmost. Be you, and you have performed your life-task in its entirety. Be you, and you will never again know despair or weakness of any kind, for no aware being of God is weak, and understanding prevents fear of all types.

Yours is the wisdom of all eternity for the humble asking and the still more humble seeking. Crawl if you must in the beginning, for surely you will walk erect and firm when your way has been opened to you. Feel in your heart the nobility of the truth and be you noble unto your last days on earth. Carry dignity upon you like a crown upon your head, and let all of your movements be cloaked with the love of all creation.

Man is not the one product of God's fertile making. All living creatures he caused to breathe and to propagate and to die in their turn. All things of earth he created for useful purposes. There was nothing made by our Lord which was

37

made wantonly, without specific reason. Many things has man turned to his own uses, twisting and distorting the true intent until it is lost from understanding.

Like fire, all parts of your world are of great benefit to mankind if used correctly and with balance. Let it be known to your heart when and how much of each is right.

Before the righteousness of the fanatic, quail not nor scorn, but rather have mercy upon the blind who will not see. In your understanding of the simple greatness of God's truth let your heart soften toward all who are unknowing and cause your greatest light of love to shine upon them.

Always, always know it is not for you to judge whether a man be right or wrong in his beliefs, right or wrong in his way of life. If you are as occupied as you should be with your own understanding and development you will have no time for criticism of others. To you who express the happy belief in the rightness of whatever destiny is marked for you goes the badge of the blessed, for you are within the kingdom of heaven. Its existence is upon the earth and all are welcome to enter who but find the gateway.

Beware that you do not also find the hell which lurks within the dark recesses of man's brain and watches its opportunity to pounce upon the mortal self with tortures beyond any possible reality. Hell exists in the physical world because man created it on that plane.

God created nothing except that which was perfect. The unknown equation of man's material being has damaged some things until they are unrecognizable in their original intent. Even the cursed scavenger has a purpose, and those who would destroy this creature are attempting to destroy God's handiwork.

Let all things live in their own way in their own surroundings. The wild beast cannot harm him who does not invade the home of the untamed. The urge to kill is turned inward in time until the killer destroys himself. So it is of the jungle law and so it is of the civilized law. You cannot hurt without hurting yourself, or destroy without destroying yourself, for you are inescapably linked to every living thing of this and other worlds. Know this and refrain with hand, with lips, and with heart from harm to any and all.

Again and again must you learn the lessons of

abhorring violence, overcoming pride and envy, banishing hatred from your heart. When these lessons are an integral part of your very being you will have passed the mark of the goal set for your attainment in life. The rewards of serenity within, of true happiness, of love and admiration are surpassed by nothing. They are your incentive to work, to study, to achieve.

Beyond the space occupied by the planet Earth waits the endless habitat of the appointed workers of God. These you can join rejoicing when you have balanced your days between receiving the light and understanding of our master within yourself, and giving of them to your fellow man.

Know that God is eternal, constant, benevolent. Know he sits not in judgment of error, or punishes by terrible means a misdeed. He alone understands always and entirely the being within and without. You have only to take his hand to know the safety of warm protection through any darkness.

Blessed is his name, for it moves the mountains and parts the seas. Blessed is his name, for it brings peace to the hearts of the turmoiled, and hope to the minds of the despairing. Blessed is his name, for it holds the light of eternal life before all and beckons toward the mighty reality of true existence.

Blessed is his name, and blessed are you who carry it within. All is God, and never shall it be otherwise than this, that he is, was, always will be.

Chapter VI

Spiritual education is like any other kind of knowledge offered for your study. First you must lay the groundwork by the most elementary methods and points of learning, then you begin applying practical approaches to simple facts. Forward you go, slowly at first, faster and faster as you are experienced more in assimilating and putting into use the knowledge you have already gained.

Each step must be put into action before the next step may be taken, for each point has its place in the whole of education and if one is missing the mind cannot jump over or go around that place.

Some students begin at an early age and seem to absorb knowledge as quickly as it is given to them. Others are slow to start and build a momentum as they go. Still others begin later and travel through their schooling at a very slow pace, but they do go through. Only the lazy or incapable cannot attain graduation eventually, whatever the speed of learning.

Spiritually, you may progress according to your individual ability and willingness much more quickly than you can materially. You are the sum of your own faith and awareness, and none can hold you back or push you forward. It lies within your own self to make your own way.

Be sure you have the faith of a little child if you would climb the mountains swiftly and surely. Believing is a form of action containing much power if you understood it more clearly. Pure trust cannot be overcome by any negative thought or action, whatever the situation. Believe you will realize God and you will. Believe you will understand his laws and you will. Believe you can actively use his power and you can. Believe you are protected by his love and you are.

Can't you see that it makes no difference what position you occupy in material life? Can't you understand that you can be more attractive to others as a simple individual who is sincere and honest than one who holds high place but hides cupidity and avarice? Can't you see you are able to travel farther as one who worries not than he who holds the fate of countries in his hands? You can be the greatest unit of ability known to your conscious mind if you will simply allow your inner being to become the ruler of your every action and your every thought.

Not one physical thing can withstand or defeat full power of an individual's spiritual being turned in that direction. You can overcome opposition of any type in business, you can secure any material possession which would add to your comfort without robbing another, you can attract all who come within the spell of yourself.

Choose carefully that which you would take for your own, person or article. If you approach all with love and confidence you will find you are in possession of the field. Give heed to the cries of others for help you can give, have mercy on those who need your mercy, be thoughtful of all who are worthy of your thoughtfulness. But do not give one step back for those who would push you aside that they might rush down a certain pathway, do not surrender meekly to those who would tread upon you in their search for personal power, do not waste time in explaining your motives to those who question them for material, selfish reasons.

Prepare to meet your God in every corner of every room, in every part of every city, in all the great outdoors, beyond the heavens of your earth. Prepare to become closer and closer to him as you walk further along the road to truth. Become cleansed of your fears and hesitancies. All of truth becomes logical as soon as you can accept that truth has been virtually unknown to the world in general and you relinquish your conventional approach to knowledge.

How can you know when truth has reached your heart at last? By the feeling of having found your home, by the deep sense of happiness and serenity which will permeate your entire being, by the swelling of your love toward all things, animal, vegetable or mineral.

Look unto the skies and they will beckon you. Listen to the winds and they will sing their sweetest songs to you. Touch the earth and it will enter you with its throbbing vitality and give you of its quality. Taste the clear purity of the water when it rains and its coolness will cleanse you from within. Smell the perfume of the flowers and be drenched in their sweet fragrance until you reflect it through your own pores.

Have always within you the sense of being alive, every moment, to the ends of your finger tips and toes. Glow with vitality until those about you are made aware of your vibrant qualities without speaking a word. Be full of the joy of living so your eyes mirror the eternal happy awareness within you and your step is as light as that of a jungle animal, who reflects his inner knowing through fearless gaze and sure gait.

Meekness is not for you who would rule your self. It is a poorly-defined word in present-day dictionaries, for its original meaning was not self-defacement but humility. No man has been expected by the mighty ones to make of himself a mat for the feet of the selfish and uncaring. To be meek is to be humble, to be gratefully aware of personal smallness while also knowing at the same time personal importance in the over-all scheme.

Servile is the present definition of meek, and it is wrong! How could such a one as God, who considers all equal, expect any to demean himself before another? There is such a difference in the intent of the ancient words and the present interpretation of them! If only those who purport themselves to be translators of the truth would add in their presentations to the world that they could be mistaken! If only they would seek the most logical meanings and stop injecting the most elaborate! If only they would understand the most impressive words are the least pompous!

There is no need for embroidery in any part of life, and particularly this is true of the wisdom of the olden days, which has been preserved until now. The more elaborate anything is made to be, the longer it is in preparation and the less understandable in action. From those who knew the truths in the time of Jesus came forth words of wisdom full of their own awareness, completely simple and understandable to all.

Simplicity should be the keynote of your life in all ways. The more simple a garment, the more attractive it looks upon the wearer. The more simple the speech, the more individuals who understand and accept it. The more simple the actions, the more honest and inspiring they show themselves to be.

God put food in abundance upon the earth for all to enjoy. In its simplest form each thing contains that which will contribute to the well-being of the physical body. Elaborately pre-pared and mixed with many other foods, it loses its greatest value, and even poisons the system when too disguised in other flavors.

There are many beautiful cloths in which to wrap the material body for shelter from the cold and the heat. Draped simply, they attract by their purity of line. Pleated, printed, flounced, tucked, they become elaborate and cheap to look upon.

All things are made more lovely by their sim-plicity. Adopt this in your life in all ways and you will find many problems have been solved by merely approaching them without elaboration. Lies will become completely unnecessary to your social activities, love will surround you on all sides, and you will be able to master any physical problem which arises. Your mind will be free of the dark doubts and fears infesting so many minds of the civilized world today. Your body will be free of the unhealthy elements contributed by the jumbled foods most individuals now consume. Your heart will overflow with happiness instead of aching with loneliness and unrequited love.

Above all, remember this: The worship of God is a simple thing also, for it is comprised of just one attribute—awareness. When you are aware of the Lord at all times, in all places and all things, you have attained the perfect worship of him in your physical body.

God is good to you who live so often in ignorant darkness. He patiently waits for your awakening to the light and treats you as others who long before found the way to him. He has no favorites and none are in disfavor with him.

May his name find its way into your consciousness as it is engraved in your heart.

Chapter VII

Harken to the sound of your own voice, calling the name of the Lord in your most desperate
moments, your greatest hours of adversity. When
your mind stops its incessant thinking and panic
erases all conscious thought, you revert to the
basic being who lives within and speaks the name
of him who always answers every call. You become
for that moment the one you should always be,
the one who knows from whence his true help
comes, the one who trusts fully in the power of
God.

Be thou alert to the strength within, the master
one who carries you across each abyss of temptation, who guards you against each act of aggression
by another, who shows you the answers to
problems which prove unsolvable in your material
world.

Look toward the heart if you would find your
self. Look toward the heart if you would know
the truth of your world. Look toward the heart

if you would understand God as he really is.

In the vast spaces of the inner being lives always the serene knowing of indestructible self, of pure faith, of power over all things within the atmosphere of the material world. Behold your real person when you would find comfort for your loneliness, courage for your fear, condolence for your sorrow. See the inner strength contain the fullest help for the outer one who so often creates situations he cannot correct alone. Seemingly impossible problems are easily conquered when you open the door to the God-self who hopes always for that opening.

Before the dawn of spiritual understanding, man is a creature of dark habits, of practices which make others miserable, but above and beyond that, which create within him a hatred and resentment ever-present and because of which he punishes others, thereby hoping to punish himself.

There has never lived an individual who was cruel or unpleasant in any manner in his material self and happily serene within his private being. The happy one can no more conceal his happiness than the light can shine without brightness. He who has found his acceptance of all life offers with eagerness and gratitude, he has found the manner of showing his fellowman love and understanding.

It is not sensible to believe a man will attempt to force upon others anything he enjoys to the utmost. He may offer to share it but he does not insist upon its being accepted. In any part of material life this can be applied as truth. He does not overwhelm by force who impresses his ways upon others, but rather does he convince by his obvious contentment and well-being.

Each man must be allowed to live according to his own personal creed. He who prays to Allah can surely live in peace beside his brother, who shouts aloud the name of Jehovah. It is only necessary that each remember to call the other one brother, and to recognize each is completely capable of choosing his own course.

He who drinks alcohol and smokes tobacco can surely enjoy recreation beside his brother, who indulges in neither. It is only necessary to remember that courtesy and consideration are as essential in leisure as in worship, and that all cannot enjoy like things.

For the favors of another individual a man

sometimes surrenders that which is his precious possession, his integrity. Once it is given away, the struggle to regain it is a long and miserable one. He should always guard his most honorable self because it is that by which he lives in harmony or exists in degradation.

Forgive your own mistakes as you would forgive those of another individual. Do not censure yourself for errors committed in the past, for they only serve to prolong the ignorance of your understanding if you persist in clinging to them. Accept that error was made, perceive the lesson illustrated by that event, go on in grateful progress from there. Give thanks you have realized the wrong turning and set your feet back upon the main road of your travel before you strayed so far you became lost.

Forget all those errors committed againt you by others who lacked their own understanding. Know they are only performing deeds which will be kept in their records for balancing before they too can find the light of their ways. Know they must correct their own mistakes as you must correct yours.

Be comforted in the knowledge that you are

marked for what you are by your own deeds. Be comforted knowing you stand or fall in the eyes of the great ones through your own efforts, that not the pushing or the pulling of any other will change your record one bit.

Forever trust that your will cannot coax you into the detours for long, or your material ego delude you into misunderstanding of self for long. This is the greatest of the facts you can take unto yourself in the beginning of your search, that nothing can prevent your finding the truth which leads to your heart for all your lifetime if you sincerely wish toward the truth.

You who feel coursing within your veins the blood of strong flow from the vital source of the universe know without explanation the reasons for your material existence, the facts of grandeur and majesty so often denied by the ignorant who cannot accept that God is simply the constant, loving being who has always been, always will be.

Speak in the language of the knowing to those who seek to learn your ways, your beliefs. Tell for the asking your faith and your understanding. If those who would know you then scoff or wish to argue, be silent and strong in your determination to speak no more and to withstand all onslaught against your beliefs.

Harm cannot be done by any individual to the part of you which is the eternal self, the God-being. No word or action can break the solid foundation of your inner one, nor can it harm the surface one if the strength from within is sufficient for outer protection.

When another would harm you physically, apply your knowledge to the victory over him. Strength beyond that of ten men is yours when your belief is ten times as great as that of your adversary.

When another would harm you socially by his vitriolic words, nullify the effect upon his listeners by smiling calmly and refusing to affirm or deny his accusations, accept or return his insults. When his words strike against an impregnable wall they can only bounce off and return to their sender.

When another would harm you spiritually by his scoffings against your own beliefs and practices, tell him you hope God goes with him always wherever he may travel, and that his heart may be peaceful with the strength of his convictions.

No man is qualified to judge another, for he is

not qualified to judge himself who has not attained complete and constant happy living. No man is qualified to preach to another what he should believe about God, for he is not qualified to preach who cannot look within himself and see the Lord smiling from deep inside the walls.

Always remember that he who steps softly, speaks quietly and only when asked to speak, helps silently without demand for gratitude, moves serenely through all days and nights regardless of outer situation, remember you — this one is that being who shows the way to you who seek the way, the one who lives the truth you wish to learn, the one who worships our Lord as he is truly worshiped by the master ones and the knowing of the more understanding worlds.

Recognize him that your path may be smoothed by his example before you, your realization quickened by his active proof of law in action. Recognize him that you may sit at his feet and listen to your own God speak through his mouth. Recognize him that you may touch him who has walked in the ways of the mighty and worshiped by their sides and sung with their voices the praise of God.

Chapter VIII

Feel my presence in the crystal clearness of a lovely spring day. Know it is the true being who is aware of the beauty permeating the body, freshening it and renewing the buoyant ability to enjoy each moment of each day.

Feel my presence in the black spell of a night when the moon sleeps behind the veil of shadows and the stars are like diamonds against a background of velvet. Know it is the basic self who is aware of the call of the darkness, awakening the physical body to alert observance of the tremendous amount of activity in the atmosphere of the night.

Feel my presence in the crisp beauty of a day in autumn. Know it is the spiritual body who is aware of the aliveness in the air, rejuvenating mind and outer body which have slowed to the tempo of summer heat, crackling with the cool touch of winter's coming sleep.

The Lord speaks thus to his subjects, his

creations, through all the changing seasons of the earth, the response of each being to those changes. He knows it is the awareness within which creates awareness without and leads unerringly to material happiness, for in active appreciation of surroundings the physical one attains happy acceptance of his destiny.

Bring to your life the full attention of your most potent ability to accept, understand and be grateful for all which you experience as you pass along the way of brotherhood, on which path tread the feet of every being who exists. See that each has a heart like your own, a soul like your own, a yearning for happiness like your own. In adversity cling you to your brother so you may give to him your strength and faith, for it is inevitable that by expressing love and a willingness to share your own belief in God's eternal help you will raise him who is in the embrace of despair and reward yourself with more of the feeling of our Lord's love for all.

Crush your own unhappy moments under the heel of your eager step toward the knowledge it is not the will of God that any man should suffer wrongly. If momentary discouragement would conquer basic faith, cling to your motto, The Lord is my shepherd, and your problems will be important no more.

Beyond the hope of the optimistic and the defeatism of the pessimistic lies the truth of the glories open to all to experience. Look beyond the edge of your property and the sun shines as brightly everywhere for others to be warmed by. Look beyond the walls of your church and the faith is as strong for those in other churches as is yours. Look beyond the horizon of your world and the spaces hold fascination for all who would explore more than the known and the seen, all who have not fear of that which is not yet understood.

Think upon the words of the Lord in the stillness of the sleep-time when others of your circle rest their physical bodies. Ponder them well in meditation when you can feel you are alone in the world of his making and man's confusing. Say them to yourself when you are alone in the midst of many and have need for reassurance that you are indeed a part of his self which is inviolable, indestructible.

The words of the Lord are these—I am all there

is to know, all there is to be. I am the cause of creation and the goal. I am the stillness of the silence and the mighty roar of the storm. I am all things and all things are nothing except they are a part of me.

Walk straight and strong, for I dwell within thee and make thee my own self. Talk true and sweetly, for I speak through thy mouth in thy real moments and make thy words felt throughout every being who hears them. Be kindly and firm, for I act in thee in thy best deeds and make thy heart sing in the doing of my will.

Bring forth every tarnished triumph and speak to your Lord, saying, I have taken this in pride and have forfeited one true triumph, Lord. Let me know the strength to pay my price with understanding and a firm knowledge that I will not again act in this manner.

Bring forth every dreary defeat and speak to your Lord, saying, I have accepted this in the false belief I must know only sorrow and despair, Lord. Let me know the joy of being my strongest self, unbending to the will of my own material mind or that of others, that I may win through faith alone the glories I have earned with my own hands.

Show your true color by reflecting you your kindliness in your eyes, your consideration in your speech, your affection in your manner, and you will blaze forth with a brilliance everlasting and overcoming.

See him who has the brightness about him at all times. Note his calm look, his quiet helpfulness, his royal bearing. Is it not enough to have before you the example of such a one to inspire you to being the same, to doing likewise? Surely in your atmosphere you have encountered a man or a woman who holds these attributes as a ruler holds a scepter and wears a crown.

The time has come to seek the leaders who have been sent to show the way to God's truth. Should you have found such a one already, ask that you may be a follower in his footsteps, for you will have fastened your heart to his heart then, and your days will be full of the glories of new, constant discoveries in the realms of the mighty current of the universe.

Do not be misled by material standards of any sort. There is beauty in every individual who bears the torch of the workers from the heavens, but often it is not that of conventional physical standards. It is however fully as visible if you will but be open to it. There is humility in every being who has the knowledge which can put you on your pathway toward fulfillment, and it is most obvious in your material world. There is wisdom in every one who is a worker for God himself, and you can find it who ask searching questions which should be answered with quiet sureness, not at all with assured superiority.

Find you a leader, you who are fortunate enough to be within touch of the hand of a mighty one, and do not lose sight of the guiding mind who is on your earth only to serve God and his fellow-beings.

Preserve always your most open attitude toward all things you hear, that you may not overlook a seemingly small item of knowledge. It might in actuality be a great fact for your development.

That which is written by Destiny is written in pencil, for the human part of man is like a deli-cately-balanced leaf in the wind. There is no foreknowledge as to which way it will blow, and that which follows must of necessity go in the direction of its going. Man chooses for himself at each crossroad, unless he has attained the happy faculty of allowing his inner being to indicate for him at all times. If such is not the case, his mind may take the wrong turning and Destiny must rewrite itself.

The future is known only partly to even the most high, since it has been freely allowed to man to accomplish or defeat his own triumph without urging in either direction. Small events even cannot be predicted with accuracy because of this instability of the human mind.

Therefore, seek not to know the ways your physical feet will travel, for too often the mind hampers your steps and causes them to stumble. Know only that it is sure you will walk in the ways of our Lord if you but seek to find those ways, that you will see by the light of our Lord if you but accept the light when it is held toward you, that you will live with the serenity of the Lord if you but understand his laws and apply them to your own life.

Remember well the words you have heard here, for they may change the course of your material existence so greatly you will become like another individual than that one in whom you have been dwelling since the beginning of your present lifetime. Seek the one who can guide you if your hand needs the clasp of another in order to climb the first steps of the mountain. Do not take it for granted he will be known by his obvious qualifications, for until the time has come that he may speak openly he works quietly and in the background for the enlightenment he so earnestly wishes to bring about.

Let him who is your guide be indicated by unmistakeable signs for your own realization, rather than the word or experience of another. Let your heart freely recognize him as one who can bring you into closer contact with the spaces of God.

Open thy being, o mortal one, that thy spirit may come forth and cause thee to live forever in the silent glories of the Lord's house for his serving and worship.

Chapter IX

Hold close within you the knowledge of your certain ascension to the heights of the hills of the Lord within your present lifetime if you continue to seek with open mind and accept with open heart those lessons which come to you. Know beyond any doubt that your personal experiences are right for you and the errors you find along your way are parallel to those committed by your material being in the learning and using of that which is taught to you in school. By trial and often by error do all learn the lessons of living, both physical and eternal.

Have close at hand the strength which will carry you beyond the sore travail with which an unknowing being's material life is often beset. Let it be your shield if you must stand still before the onslaught of terrific force from worldly causes, let it be your spear if you must win free of a trap in which you are caught temporarily. Know your strength can grow to any proportion as it is needed and can survive any test thought of in the mind of mortal man.

Call upon the God within you at any hour of the day or night. Call him for the purpose of asking help, of giving thanks, of seeking knowledge, or simply of speaking with your closest friend. He is ready to listen always, and in the simple conversations you learn to enter with him at intervals during the day he will answer you with serenity and a release from any tension. In the night's stillness his consciousness comes into your material mind like the open winds of the mountains, like the smallest part of the earth. Cling to him in silence while the world sleeps and he fills you with the height and greatness of knowing beyond any question he is indeed within, a part of you and as much a part of you as your own hands or feet.

The Lord exists as surely and as tangibly as physical things of your world. You have only to become aware that this is so to realize the knowledge has been before you always and it has been your own preoccupation with the activities of material living which blinded you to the greatest fact of your atmosphere. He is all about you, for your eyes to see from birth — the loveliness of all nature is his creation for your enjoyment, your fellow beings are his also, for you to look upon and marvel that such a seemingly complex mechanism could be produced so simply.

God surrounds you at all times with beauty of one kind or another, and when you can be actively aware of this beauty every waking moment you will have secured for yourself a step upon the rung of the ladder running well beyond the lower footpath by which the unknowing climb the mountain.

Fill the cup of heaven for your own drinking in the study and practice of the basic truths of your universe. They are the same truths upon which all other worlds were built and yours is the same eternal being which dwells in all beings.

The truths are simple, for all basic greatness is simple. There are no mazes in which the bewildered can be lost, no hazards in which the unwary can perish. Let your mind know these things are so and you shed like the magic cape of an enchanting one the foolish superstitions and dark beliefs clinging to your conscious self and frightening it into immobility.

First, know your God. Know, though you cannot understand his form or features, that he is all-good, all-loving, all-benevolent. Know he would not smite in anger or punish in judgment. Know he understands all and always. Know he has within himself the power times beyond counting more than dwells within you, and realize your lesser ability can conquer any part of the physical plane of existence. With this mighty power then would the Lord have need of anger or resentment or any of the lesser qualities of man, qualities which are in reality emotions? He has no use for emotion, only for love.

All-encompassing is his love for all things of his creation, so our God has created one basic law ahead of all others — he who harms willfully or destroys willfully another of God's creations, be it human, animal or plant, so shall he be harmed to a like degree or destroyed within himself.

None shall decree, "I am God," and take into his own hands the dispensing of another's destiny, for though it is true he is God he has not the one thing withheld by our Lord from other hands — the power to create or destroy physical life. In his mighty wisdom God knew the consequences of investing authority in the physical man who walks the earth and all other planets. He knew the weakness of personal lust for importance would in most instances be a strength big enough to overcome the small voice from within.

The basic law states that all shall love all others of creation, even unto the last blade of grass.

Also states the basic law that a balance shall be maintained in the universe, in the world, in each individual. When any activity is performed the record writes of it that at some future date the balance may be regained through a righting action. To give tilts the balance wheel until a gift has been received. To take will require a giving. To love will call forth love in return, while to perform an act of hate or resentment will send back in time a sad event of like magnitude.

That which you receive without force upon your part is that to which you are due. You need feel no qualms of conscience if your material worth is greater than that of your neighbor, for paid by your own hands is the winning of advancement of any kind and your neighbor must also pay for his own.

Help all you can him who is without the

material means for living in cleanliness and comfort within your atmosphere, but do not allow one who is as the leech to attach himself to your being, for in sucking the power of your help he will be robbing you of understanding. You cannot toil for another along the path of life, nor shall you lead him by the hand who wants only to ride without charge upon your back. Give of yourself and of your goods to assist those who have felt the bite of adversity, make an opening for them if you can and will that they may find their way once again, but do not eagerly support that one who is lazy in his heart and sluggard by nature.

The basic law states that any extreme is not to be endured nor is it to be condoned. Too much is as distasteful as too little, and after a man has reached the point of supply for all his needs and comforts, let him give of the rest to those who have not yet found their opportunity for material wealth. If a man is in the midst of want let him look to himself for the reasons. He can win out of these surroundings if he will simply find his true being and listen to its wise voice, for it will guide him into the light of worldly happiness.

God intended the world to be peopled by happy, active beings who were perfectly balanced between their material and actual selves. There is food in abundance for all upon the earth. There are garments for all to wear, shelters for all from the tempests. Each one has his place in the order of things if he will but find it. There is no one born into the material world who is lost and without assignment. Let him know his work by the answer coming to him from the stillness of meditation and inner seeking.

All unhappiness, all misery is man-created and man-sustained. The terrors of the unknown are developed through man's deliberate letting go of his inner knowledge many centuries ago, when the material gold before his eyes began to glitter more brightly to him than the gold of the inner truths which he could only see by turning away from the gold for which he lusted.

Illness is a product of man's miserable practices also. He who has the truth shining always before him is in good state though the air be cold with freeze or hot with tropical sun. He walks through the pestilence of disease and is untouched, he treads the shadows of crime-ridden streets and is unharmed, he enters dark holes and travels perilous trails and is well.

The Lord is the shepherd of all who will accept him completely. Let your will be silent and your willing be ascendant if you would find his strength within you and his protection about you.

Worship in the silence of hallowed thoughts and the thunder of great crowds, worship wherever you are, at whatever task you toil. Worship by being alive every moment of every day, by being alert every second of every night. Even as you sleep shall you worship who wish to do so. Even as you work shall you worship who know happiness in your labor. Even as you perform any daily activity shall you worship who accept that you are God and God is you, to the most distant point of your existence, the beginning and the end of your days.

Lord, Lord, thy name is a glory overcoming in its saying!

Chapter X

Bright are the stars above your head in the night when you are opened to the cry of the night-bird and the sound of the tree-whispers in your ears. Full of the joy of living is your being when you are conscious in every pore of the dancing beams of the sun by day, and the whirling activity of the atmosphere as the earth goes about its business of fulfilling its destiny.

Breathe deep of the air that you may fill your physical body with cleansing and vibrant currents. This is not the act of a mere exercise for your lungs, but a ritual of emptying the channels of the inner organs of their waste and filling them with the new, wine-like oxygen provided in the surface areas of the planet.

You can step forth each morning with a smile on your lips, wings on your feet and a song in your heart. Accomplish the understanding of inner you and allow it full expression. Transcend momentary distractions through the power of your faith in the will of the Lord. Act in kindness, speak in friendship, help in the name of God.

Believe beyond question you are an entire unit in yourself. Know the universe is as much yours as it is claimed in the names of the mighty ones. See within your own self the power to maintain the balance of your life and the triumph of your goal.

Basically, God has stated the universe hangs upon the slender thread of the slightest thought of any one individual, and upon the strong rope of the mightiest deeds of all beings of creation. Let this be at once your comfort in moments of material loneliness and your governor in impulses of selfishness or cruelty.

Chapter XI

How shall you live your days in the expression of your faith and understanding? Believe in the power of the Lord's will to bring into your atmosphere those things earned by your work and effort toward the full realization of creation. Accept all events in the happy knowing they are but lessons in your school of understanding, stones put before your feet to test the sureness of your step. Look to the light of God's strength for deliverance from miserable mistakes, for achievement of material goals, for fulfillment of human happiness in the heart.

Make the most of each moment of your physical life by tending the tasks for your material self to perform while concentrating within your inner being on the declarations of faith, power and love to be found in every moment, every thought of your world.

Knot the strength of your soul and the willingness of your body together and you have tied

75

an unbreakable bond which will bring forth complete serenity and happiness regardless of your outer duties. These forces combined are the sum of material existence at its peak and they are the only weapons needed to win the success, admiration and contentment so easy to reach for the knowing.

Practically, the force of God can do anything in the physical world. It can create situations, change them, or abolish them completely. It can touch the least one with the light of inspiration and change him into a leader among men. It can humble the mightiest, deflate the proudest, beautify the plainest, uplift the most despairing. By the will of the Lord seeming miracles are created, and all his creatures are awed and wondering at his might. So goes the power within all beings, ever-present and ready, only waiting for awareness and active application to express itself to any degree desired. Without limit is God, without limit is his ability, without limit is his love.

Go beyond the boundaries of the mind if you would find the key to this power. Go into the silence and find your self if you would know how to use your power. Then go out of yourself completely for the sake of your fellow beings if you would experience the full flow of your power. Self-control is the beginning of your search for mastery, self-seeking the next step, and self-effacement the final application of your understanding.

To make dormant, placid the material mind is not always an easy task for those of the physical plane who have made a daily habit of constant worrying. It is well worth the effort when complete relaxation of the body has been accomplished and the mind ceases to whirl with cares.

The next step, self-seeking, self-understanding, likewise is not easy, for a simple fact is difficult for the material being to accept. That you are God himself, with a material covering of his creating, is a statement of truth, but do you accept it without a thousand questions immediately dizzying your mind? The inner one is serene, knowing, undoubting. That being you will be happy to know, for it will no doubt surprise you to learn *you* are a much better individual than you had ever believed you were. Give yourself the credit of being good within your deepest parts, then you will be ready for the next step.

Self-effacement is not an expression of complete servility. It is the ability to forget ego entirely in the effort to help others, materially or spiritually. It is a desire to share God-knowledge with fellow beings, a feeling of such love and oneness as to overwhelm the material self until it does not exist for that moment. Give of yourself to all who come your way, for it is a privilege to serve in the name of the Lord those who need your services.

Temper your giving with an intelligence of a like degree. Give all you have to give of your understanding, your faith, your power in order to help those who would find their way to God, but withhold your secret self from the grasping, the greedy, the evil. To give of your heart does not include giving of your material self. To give of your time does not include giving of all your days to one individual who is selfish. To give of your knowledge does not include giving of your every thought to one who would attach himself to you because his own will is too weak to be of use to him.

Always maintain a balance, even though you

go about the Lord's work. He does not expect any individual to sacrifice his dignity or his self-respect for the sake of another. He asks only that you give of your best, all of it, without including your surface being.

In offering help to the grieving, do not shed tears for the sorrow of another. Detached sympathy will accomplish far more in comforting than a sharing of weeping. Emotion causes tears to flow, and the Lord's intent cannot be done with emotion. It requires a calm, all-loving but impersonal approach to be completely effective.

In offering assistance to the despairing, do not acquire the worries of another. To absorb into your own mind another's problems is to reach the same level of desolation. The presence of faith is impossible if the mind is actively engaged in worldly affairs.

Give of your time, give of your understanding, give of your knowledge. Give all you possess and you will be richer for the giving instead of poorer, for it is written that he who shares all he has with his fellow man shall then receive more than that which he gave. Give not in the expectation of reward, either material or heavenly, but rather for the exalted joy of giving. There is no soul-satisfaction equal to that which follows the offering of all you have to offer.

So you shall give all the days of your life, and they shall be like the locusts in their number and in their full happiness. Like the beams of the sun dancing through the air shall be the joys which come to you in the fulfillment of your destiny and of your expression of love for all.

Hear in your secret ears the voices of the angel choir when your own voice sounds with words of kindness to one who stands before you. Speak with nothing but love in your heart and you will endure the words of vicious ones with patience and understanding, for knowledge brings an armor against ignorance and turns away its ugly rays as though they were nonexistent.

Raise your inner sight to the glories of the heavens when you look upon a fellow being, whether he be beautiful to the physical sight or unpleasant to view. See only his image mirroring your own within the outer casing, and know in his heart he has the same longings, the same pulsebeat, thc same great God.

How can any man be less than you or more, when all possess the same one? Surface ignorance cannot disguise the greatness of any soul if your own is discerning. Surface arrogance cannot disguise the humble self of any being if your pride is subdued completely. Surface indifference cannot disguise the hunger for love and understanding of any human creation if your heart is great enough to realize the identical longings within each heart.

Subdue your material, surface self if you would understand the outer selves of those you encounter in everyday living. Control the critical attitude of your mind toward appearances, actions, words of others. There is no excuse for the knowing to express derision or to misunderstand motives. It is your responsibility to express your awareness at all times, in all ways. That you sometimes forget and slip into the ways of your human self is an indication of the distance you still must travel to attain your goal.

Love the Lord thy God in all his ways and in all his intentions. Obey his will in all thy days and in all thy deeds. Make his laws thy creed and thy passion. Thou shalt be exalted to the spaces of the great ones in thy own day and beyond shalt thou find the crops thou didst reap in thy sowing on earth.

Chapter XII

God is good to those who believe in him night and day, for their own belief brings forth his strength, waiting within, coming to its destined fulfillment with the expression of pure faith at all times.

In the operation of the God-power possessed by all lies the explanation of seeming feats of incredible strength, of accomplishments beyond the average material ability, of forbearance during times of such trial as to bring forth doubt of the humanity of man.

Like trees growing along a river, beings gain their nourishment from the mighty waters rushing by, beneath and within them. The river flows underground and makes its liquid self a part of the tree roots that they might be sustained in their seeking to live. So does the presence of God permeate the roots of every being, giving them a ripeness, a fullness which cannot be known without awareness of the source of all ability, all good things of the physical world.

Believe in the power and the presence of the Lord within your own being and you will accomplish everything you are longing to accomplish, attain all you wish to attain. The one factor needed for entire happiness, complete serenity, unchanging contentment, is faith. Only good can come from a true belief in God, for God is not anything less than good in his own self.

Less than perfection is possible only to material beings, not to the Lord. He is perfect in all ways, with not one emotion to mar his loving benevolence, with no dark thoughts to unfasten the mighty chain of his eternal existence. He is the ultimate in love, the goal of all creation, the focal point of the human heart.

Behold the light of God in the rainbow across a sky. Its beauty is never dimmed by time, by constant sightings. Its colors are as bright as those of the first rainbow ever sighted by man, so long ago the exact time has been lost in the dim shadows of antiquity. Indestructible are all things of God's true creation, and by this you may measure those matters most desirable to your mind at present and always during your material lifetime.

Do not dissipate your most powerful thoughts and efforts on things which are of little standing in the eyes of the mighty, of small importance in your eternal existence. The admiration of individuals who pass by on the fringe of your atmosphere is a most unimportant accomplishment, not worthy of your conscious striving, and automatically assured you anyway if you are living by the laws of which you are aware.

Elaborate foods are not necessary to the maintenance of your physical body or even desirable to keep it at a point of maximum efficiency. They are more costly than the simple, healthier edibles and are sometimes a goal of gross importance to those who consider eating one of the major purposes in existing.

All things of the material world can be likened to these examples. The clothes you wear, the social circles you choose, the activities in which you indulge, all are a part of your life but not more than a part. They are not the end of any attainment, any striving for success. As you live so shall you die, for in death as it is known to the physical plane emerges life in its true meaning. You will go on in your true body as you have acted in your material being, the pattern having been set by your actions during this lifetime.

No one can escape his own mistakes or his own accomplishments. He must correct the one before he can go on upon the path destiny marks for him, and he will be paid in returns of gold for each golden deed of his days on earth. This is a comfort to the knowing, that the mistakes of others in which innocent ones may have been embroiled shall be accounted for only by him who has made the mistake. It lies in a man's attitude and reactions to life whether he shall reap rewards for his valor or drudge to erase his cowardice. The experiences with which he is faced are unimportant except as lessons for his eternal self, as steps on his path to understanding.

You cannot judge how a man shall react to any situation, for yours is an individual experience and so is his, so are all others. You can wish him well, help him if you are able, but criticize or advise you cannot—not in honesty and with ability. You are qualified only to offer your inner knowledge to him who asks it of you, to offer your loving understanding to him who needs a hand to which to cling, to offer your material experience to him who is working with material objects.

Do not confuse the desire to be of assistance to all with the human failing of believing you are qualified to judge how much assistance you can give.

Good intentions are not an excuse for a mistake such as you would be making if you told another of his faults in the hope you were inspiring him to correct them. That which is a fault in your eyes may be an endearing trait in the eyes of another. It is not your concern whether a man has habits needing correction. It *is* your concern to attain a kindly, uncritical attitude toward all, regardless of material idiosyncrasies. Remember, you too are a human being and undoubtedly have mannerisms which are irritating to the disapproving.

The surface characteristics of an individual are a sure indication of the extent of his awareness. There are many who exercise their abilities contained within, many with a complete unconsciousness of the power they use. To him who knows what lies in every breathing thing it is a natural, almost mechanical habit to express the God of which he is so conscious. Courtesy becomes as much a part of his actions as drawing a fresh breath every few moments. Kindliness becomes as much a part of his attitude as putting one foot in front of the other in order to walk. Thoughtfulness becomes as much a part of him as the beat of the heart which motivates his actions to the almost complete exclusion of conscious inclinations.

Look for the individual who exercises these characteristics at all times and you have found him who can speak to you of things beyond the general knowledge of man. Look for the one who unconsciously maintains a constant thoughtfulness of others and you have found him who can tell you of the ways of loving as God would have them followed.

In the ways of the Lord shall you find the fulfillment of all your unnamed longings, all your suppressed feelings toward happiness in the material world.

It is not the purpose of your existence that you should deny yourself the comforts of physical things or the expression of physical inclinations. It is intended that you should find and maintain a balance in order to live your days with contentment and purpose.

To pretend your heart does not cry out for the love of another being is like covering your eyes from the noonday sun and proclaiming it is night. God would not have created the material hunger for affection if it had no place in your life. To withhold from all pleasures of the world and call them sinful is like tying your own hands and proclaiming it was done by force againt you. God would not have created music and dancing and laughter if they had no use in your life. To say of the Lord that he wishes you to live in poverty, privation, complete self-denial, is to preach against his mighty all-loving, all-goodness, all-understanding, all-knowing.

There is no extreme in the material world created by other than man himself. God is the perfect balance of all things, and such is the pattern by which he made the universe.

Love the Lord thy God with joy, not in fear of his reprisals for your very thoughts. Worship the Lord thy God with happiness, not in loud proclamation that he may not hear the voice of your unbelief. Trust the Lord thy God with love, not in half-resentment of his power.

Know the Lord thy God with all of thy being, for thou then knowest thyself and in self-understanding dost thou know all others of creation.

Let the light of truth mark thy steps through every night and the stroke of each hour shall bring thee closer to the mount of everlasting existence.

Chapter XIII

Fill yourself with the glory of God's existence, of his presence, of his power. Use your faith in the execution of the humblest of your daily tasks, the most exalted of your privileged activities. Believe in him who must exist or you yourself would have no existence, trust in him whose hands are always kindly and warm and strong, turn to him who has the true answer to any question troubling your heart. Let not your mind, a material thing, interfere with the reverent awareness of your self, with the acceptance within your being of that which God decrees for your steps through physical life.

Behold the father of the universe in your own marvelous material body. Its functions are so intricate even your greatest scientists cannot explain them all. Behold the mother of the universe in the pattern of propagation, whose secret juices cannot be duplicated in the most elaborately equipped laboratories. Behold the beginning and the end of the universe in the glory of a sunrise and the serenity of a sunset, the tides of the seas and stillness of small pools.

Calm but overwhelming is all experience within God's universe if the being can but attain understanding of all motives, acceptance of all events, gratitude for all learning. To know is to understand. To understand is to accept, and to accept is to be grateful. Step by step can anyone attain this perfect balance in a world full of material barriers to serenity, but step by step must the goal be won.

The seemingly little things of your material life are those upon which the foundation of your very soul is built. The rock-base or the sand-floor are created by the pounding of the surf in your world, the waves constantly throwing at your feet for discovery or rejection the precious stones or empty shells of earth's atmosphere. You alone can learn to distinguish which is of value to you and which worthless, for that stone you would pick up and take with you always would be like a piece of gravel to him who has no awareness of precious stones or is beyond the edges of the rocks.

Be aware of living in every small day, for in

the eternal kingdom's records there are no small days in your lifetime upon the planet of the mortal ones. Each is a step in your development, a drop of water in the huge bowl of your fulfillment. Know when you awaken in the cool of morning that God smiles at you while you prepare for a humble task, just as he smiles upon your bowed head when you work in his name upon your soul. Know when you rest in the still of the evening that God smiles at you for the completion of your most mundane duties, just as he is touching you in blessing when you have offered your hand to another in love and understanding.

It is not the duty of the average human being to live the supreme life of one like Jesus or Buddha. Few are equipped to maintain such a high level of awareness, and the forcing of effort toward this height can only harm without any beneficial results. Maintain your own level in honesty, in happiness, in constant awareness of what you are. God's blessings are upon him who humbly is that which he was intended to be. It is not right that a man whose work in the material world is to guide the ignorant toward the doorway to understanding should instead live as a recluse

in a lonely spot and spend his days in contemplation of the skies. It is not right that a man whose
work is to serve materially should denounce all
things of the conscious plane and attempt to live
the life of an ascetic.

Like the flow of waters toward the sea, left
alone to pursue its course without barriers, your
life stream will travel in the proper direction and
with the right amount of speed. You need have
no worries as to its destination and no qualms as
to its course. Swim with your personal current
and it will carry you into the ocean of happy
living.

While the heart is sore with loneliness when
no one apparently shares the day's duties or cares
about the longings within, remember this: The
Lord has made his workers to be aware of all
things, and this is not the least of their concerns
but one of the greatest, for it is written that no
man shall exist without feeling the love of other
beings, nor shall he pass through his lifetime without feeling the outpouring of his love for others.
Like all things of your pattern, love fits in where
it should, at the right time, in the proper place.
Should you be without the closeness of another

for what seems to you long periods of time, know it is best you should be. Accept without understanding until understanding comes to you, and following will be serenity of heart in the knowledge you have not been cheated of your rightful possessions or experiences.

Whatever lack you see within your own atmosphere is no lack unless you have forced the road into a wrong turning. That which is yours by right will be yours as surely as the sun covers the day, so long as yours is a willing step and not a forceful, willful wandering. Take what you will, if you are agreeable to paying the price for balancing your destiny again after the taking. Be headstrong if you will, if you cannot believe the mighty ones are wiser than you in knowing what is best for your knowing.

But if you truly believe the Lord is your shepherd, if you fully accept that your destined path is full to the brim with the waters of joyful living, then cultivate patience in all things and in all ways for the passing of time until material realizations are yours. Time is as fleeting as the glimpse of a star shooting across the heavens, and though day by day it crawls as a snail, year by year it carries on wings through your consciousness until all time has passed and you are once again at the beginning of your awareness.

Let go of avarice, for when you possess all the wealth your arms can hold your heart will still be empty. Let go of envy, for when your mind is poisoned with jealousy of that which belongs to another your eyes will be blinded to the beauties before them. Let go of fear, for when your body has turned to water at the sight of that which confronts you your faith will die within you and crumple into dust even as your knees crumple beneath you.

Find your own way, not that of your neighbor, but always remember to allow him his way also. You would not have him walk your path, which is wide enough for only one, and you would not walk with him, for his way would be strange to you. Live kindly, with understanding of the motives beneath the unkindnesses of others. Live generously, with no thought of return in material ways for your deeds and only joy in the ability to give. Live thoughtfully, with courtesy always toward those you encounter, servant or ruler, and with the knowledge uppermost within you that here too stands a human being.

Live with joy, with full happiness, with God freed within you to express the mightiest gestures of his love toward all creation. Show in your face the awareness to which you cling, show in your step the freedom to which you aspire, show in your touch the soft compassion to which you hold in all your dealings.

The knowledge of God's true intent is a practical knowledge, for in its full use you can accomplish anything materially and everything spiritually. It is all you need for complete success in any field, complete victory in any contest, complete fulfillment in any longing.

Do not be afraid to act as a human being, for that is what you are, that is what the Lord created you to be. A human being is more than a physical body and material mind. He is the expression of God himself, the external expression of the inner awareness. Combine your marvelous physical attributes with your perfect spiritual attributes and you will have become the human being God intended you to be when he caused you to exist. Do not hesitate to sing, to dance, to love the choice of your heart. Also, do not hesitate to give of your self in the name of the Lord, to help him who has become lost, to share your riches with him who has none. You should not give all of your self in any way, and in this lies the balance which equals ideal living.

The only prayer you will ever have need of is that of asking the Lord to help you to acceptance and understanding of his ways with you. He and his workers will do the rest. You have only to open your heart and he will show you your soul.

Chapter XIV

Built by master hands is the universe and all
that lies beyond. So have been built the most
infinitesimal insects and the hugest creatures
of earth. So have been built the light of the
moon and the heat of the sun, crispness of
autumn days and smell of summer flowers.
Likewise have the human body and the human
brain been constructed, on lines of greatness, a
pattern of beauty. None can say the physical
body is ugly and speak in truth, for the Lord
created nothing repulsive to look upon. None
can say the mind is a trap of devious routes
for the unwary or uncaring, for the Lord made
the mind of man to be his messenger from his
soul to the outer surface of his being.

All about lies the proof of God's existence,
of his abilities, of his might. Open yourself to
these truths and you will overcome the shadows
of your material cares, the valleys of your
material dangers. The Lord within you can

protect you from all onslaught if you are but free of physical emotions when facing your adversaries. He has no fear himself, therefore he created your inner self without fear. Overcome your worries and your cowardice with the warm protection of faith in the strength of God.

First of all your duties in the material world is the execution of your daily tasks, with happiness in accomplishment of these matters to your best ability. The act of performing those things you must tend to is an act of expressing your faith in the rightness of God's chosen path for you.

Second of your duties is the expression of love on all sides, in all directions, though you are sorely oppressed with cupidity, avarice, hatred from without. You can even then bring forth the love from within at such strength it will overcome the enemy emotions trying to conquer you.

Win you the respect, the admiration, the affection of every individual in your atmosphere by an unfailing courtesy, an unchanging control, an obvious warmth exuding from your eyes and your attitude. There can be no mistaking your motives when you express honesty always. There can be no misunderstanding of your meanings when you speak truly always. There can be no misinterpreting of your actions when you treat all in fairness at all times.

Here in the heart of you lies the kernel of truth, simple, healthy, vibrant, always ready to spring forth into a growing and blooming at the first drop of water from the stream of your awakened consciousness. Trust in the Lord and all things find their proper place as the movements of Nature are in their proper order. Turn to the certainty within you of the ultimate realization of your pattern when you have need of answer to "why?" Melt the icy covering over your awareness and you will succeed in reaching a peak of happiness beyond the attainment of those who strive entirely in a material phase of activity.

When the truth has reached you in such strength as to overwhelm all doubt and fear you will cease your impatient waiting for events of which you dream. You will at once stop your calling upon God to lighten his punishment, for you will understand he does not judge; nor does he punish in any way at any time. You will touch the hand of him with whom you come into contact and feel you are but touching your own.

Seek the serenity waiting within you. It is well worth the trouble and the time of searching. It glows always through the darkness of your misery if you can only lift your eyes slightly above the dreary pictures before you. It protects you from the ravages of physical combat, whether it be a duel of minds or a battle between countries.

Look for the signs of your approaching understanding. Can you take one day, that in which you are at present active, and live that day for its sake alone? Can you take your neighbor, he who is nearest you at present, and give him your love in some manner, whether it be a favor, a business agreement or an apology? Can you take the delay before happy material realizations and utilize it for the purpose of studying the spaces of the universe or understanding the unimportance of time or preparing your balance to meet overwhelming events with equanimity?

You who can do these things are well upon your way to the goal of constant self-control, constant awareness, constant love for all creation. Let it be your creed to walk in silence among the noisy, to sit in reverence among the unbelieving, to kneel in humility among the egotistical. The last must be done in the secret places of the heart and not in physical movement, for the proud would then deride and become more proud, thus soiling the purity of your motives.

Believe at all times in the sweetness of life and the glory of death. Believe though all your worldly affairs have gone awry and you stand seemingly alone before the barriers rising to heights beyond your vision. Believe when your eyes pour forth tears of despair and your hands are helpless to pull you from the depths of material desolation. Believe though the blackest of nights has descended about you and your way is unknown to you at that moment.

It is in the faith you cling to during such moments that your true power is generated and your path straightened out in its true direction. If you can believe the Lord intends nothing but good for you, that he plans always for your happiness, your successful destinations in life though all about you are seeming material indications the opposite is true, then shall you know the secrets of his universe in all their parts. You shall know the guarded knowledge living beyond the boundaries of the human mind. You shall know the glories held by the mighty ones in hands always ready to open to the honest seekers.

It is simple to give in to despair, to give up to mistakes, to give out only hatred and resentment. Strong is the one who casts despair into the spaces beyond danger, who conquers the desire to stop trying because errors have been made, who holds no malice toward enemies and no discourtesy to the rude.

You must be strong if you would reach the end of your path in the present lifetime with the banner of triumph flying above your head. There is no room for weakness in any phase of living, either on your planet or in the planes beyond. To the strong shall go the rewards of life, the realizations of eternal living. To the strong shall go the ability to succeed, the talent to produce, the capacity to experience great love. None shall know the glories of the heavens and of the earth but the courageous and the undaunted. Long shall his name be spoken by the lips of the great ones who speaks softly, steps firmly, acts rightly.

Place your record in the book of those especially marked for great destinies by refusing to give in to any negative thought, action or person. There can be no avoiding unpleasant situations so long as the world remains in its present state of exaggerated materialism, but your reactions are more important than the situations with which you are confronted, and your actions are more important than the ultimate results. Jesus was a great being because he truly practiced the laws of God in his attitude and his actions. It is of little importance that he died as a criminal was made to die, that he was humiliated in the eyes of the ignorant on his way to death. What lives beyond the event of his dying is his great faith in the Lord who created him even as you were created.

Find your courage in the words of God who says: Should thy blood turn to water and thy bones melt away, still will I be with you and of you always. Should the ways of your world become those of an alien land and unknown to your longings, still will I stand by to give to you of my knowing and my comfort. Should you wait alone for the beauty of the sunrise and the twilight of your days, still will I accompany you on every journey, be it to view the rising sun or to meet the eternal world beyond your grave.

Embrace the Lord unto your closest self, beyond the embracing of any other, and you will have called unto you the greatest love man can know. Take his truths unto your innermost thoughts, beyond the knowledge found in any book, and you will have found the key to understanding beyond the locks of any material doors.

Be true to your self and you are true to him who created you. Be wise in his ways and you are through your search for contentment. Reach the heights of his love and you are embraced forever in the protection of the almighty God.

Chapter XV

Take an apple from the tree and peel its skin away. Exposed will be the feeling, living essence of the fruit, vulnerable to your attack upon it, the destruction which is imminent. Likewise remove from a human being the outer armor of his pride and ego and you will find the true individual, strong or weak according to his development, exposed before your seeking eyes to read at will.

If you would know another, look beyond the surface habits, words, mannerisms. Study his expression at unguarded moments, his reactions to involuntary events, his words in unwary speeches. Watch his hands when he touches a small animal, his mouth when he looks at a child, his eyes when he sees a lame beggar. Know your fellow human beings by their true intent and not that which they would have you believe.

Also, let you yourself be known to them by

your unguarded activities. You need fear no one, man or woman, if you but look honestly into the eyes from your soul. You can conquer any situation if you but approach it openly and honestly, acting as a being of integrity and not one of cupidity. You will pass any test of strength if you but place your fate in the hands of God and then do your utmost to conquer with honor.

Behold the man without honor who seeks only material possessions and then clasps them to himself in such a clutch that eventually he strangles himself with his own holdings. Behold the man without honor who seeks material power to such a degree he is willing to bring others to degradation and ruin in order to achieve his position of might. Behold the man without honor who seeks material possession of another without true love to purify and glorify the relationship. In these you can recognize the failures of life who may be the successes of civilized living.

To him who is humble, honest and loyal often goes the task of maintaining his lofty ideals and actions in the midst of transgression, oppression and ridicule. To him let it be known he is indeed smiled upon by the great workers of the Lord and to him shall go the richest rewards in your universe, the prizes to be found in eternal existence and understanding, in material happiness after the enemy has been overcome.

No one has a passive role upon the planet Earth. To each are assigned certain duties and tasks, to be accomplished successfully or not according to the free will of the individual. There is a whole world of difference between passive acceptance of whatever confronts one and a happy acceptance of the challenging days on earth. The faith-full will make efforts to achieve the goals, finish the duties, realize the lessons of our Lord's will. The weak will call their helplessness by the name of faith and proclaim it is the Lord's will that they are poor or sick or in disgrace or without friends.

Understand always that within you yourself lies the ability to secure all the material world has to offer anyone or to be cheated of any part of the riches. You who succeed will have accepted a failure as one of the hazards along your way and go on seeking still to the heights of your goal. You cannot possibly finish anything if you are stopped by the signals before you come to the end of your road.

Like traffic in your civilization is life itself. You will have to drive carefully, pause to allow others to cross your path, stop for a rest frequently and for longer periods when the red light shows, stop to refuel your system for the journey, watch out for reckless individuals, keep your eyes constantly on the road you travel, and realize that the more solitary your journey the faster and safer it becomes. You do not attempt to drive a car two or three abreast with friends, and so do you not attempt to understand your own soul or to conclude your own traveling by sharing your inner self with others.

When you are told that it is the Lord's rule to give yourself completely to anyone who needs your help, it does not mean you are to spend day and night with that person, to tell every thought, express every feeling, give every part of knowledge you possess. It *is* intended you pour forth the full strength of your love in attitude, to give forth the full strength of your current of God-power in your touch, to show the full strength of your faith in your words and actions. Keep secret and untouched that part of you which is always alone with God and cannot be shared with anyone else. It can be exposed, but it is a sensitive, remarkable portion of the innermost you and was not meant to be made known to any except God himself. Those who understand would not seek to look upon your deepest self and those who do not understand would only think you mad if you spoke of it.

No, keep the most sacred parts of your being to yourself. Let the world see as much as it wishes of the things it can understand — your faith, your happiness, your acceptance, your courtesy, your consideration for all others. Though not all will understand these qualities, you will impress all with them and leave an indelible mark which will in time produce a reaction of great help to the individual exposed.

God has been and always will be, therefore your manifesting of this fact without any doubt whatsoever will inspire others to the same understanding in time. Some cannot understand how he exists without interfering in wars, crimes, cruelties between human beings. By acting as a station for his laws and lessons you will become one of the beacon lights in the darkness of the material world.

When your mind has ceased its constant worrying of a thought until despair sets in over belief, you will have found the path to the true faith waiting in your heart. That today there is not enough money for your obligations or anyone to accompany you upon a fearful journey means nothing, for the next day will be one of bright sunshine, with more than enough for material needs and a circle of friends from which to choose a companion for any venture. Each day is a complete cycle in itself, but no two cycles are ever exactly the same and in this can lie your comfort when despair threatens at the door of your thoughts again.

The flooding of your atmosphere with possessions, experiences, happiness of every physical kind, can be just as overwhelming as adversity. Sometimes it is more so because the average human being now meets reverses with an I-expected-it attitude, while good fortune comes so unexpectedly it cannot be handled with calm and self-control.

Be prepared at any time for any event in your

life-stream. If it is an adversity, know there is within it some gain to be found, a lesson, a new friend, a step to better conditions, something beyond the dreary picture in focus. If it is a beneficent event, know it is something you have earned by your efforts, accept it with thanks for your blessings, humility for the opportunity to savor such happiness, and sincere hopes that others may also share in your good fortune.

Reach the height of your potential ability to enjoy life by knowing you are not perfect and are not expected to be at present. You are expected to be honest, to be thoughtful at all times, to be true to your self, and to give of your love in all its degrees at the times when it is needed. Above all, cling to your faith, regardless of that which may be done to you by enemies, that which may be said to you by the malicious, that which may befall you in the course of living among other human beings.

The Lord provides all that is needed by anyone for full living. He also provides all that is needed by anyone for full appreciation of the existence beyond your physical death. Let his will guide you always and his love shine upon your head like the beam of a giant searchlight through a window. Know he has intended happiness for your physical self and find it in the willing search along your own pathway. Know he plans great joys for your spiritual self in the spaces beyond your dimension and understand these joys by opening your inner eyes to all the signs about you of his mighty power.

Bend the rod but it will not break in thy hands, o mortal, for it is made of metal such as thy physical eyes have never seen or shall ever see. Touch the heart of a flower but do not expect to learn the riddle of its existence with thy hands, for it is created from the might of one such as thy mortal touch shall never know.

This canst thou know, however, in all thy mortal days and nights — Thou art warm in the cold of ice and snow, for the Lord is with thee and will hold thee close to his protection. Thou art protected from the burning suns of deserts and tropics, for the Lord keeps thee in his shade and nourishes thee with his love. Give him only thy trust and he will give thee all the world in which thou hast existence, all the love of which thou hast dreamed, all the fulfillment to which thou wouldst cling in the final reaches of the Great Experiment.

Give thy self and he will give himself. This is the reward beyond matching, beyond price, beyond the clouds of heaven.

———————

To you, my messenger, I give this personal notice:

In the heart are many rooms, each with a name upon its door. If thou dost look within and find an empty room despair not, for in thy time shall every room have its occupant and thy house shall be full before death finds thee smilingly waiting for him.

Thy heart is full with the love of God, of thy children, of all those with whom thou dost come in contact. Seek thou and look as hard as thou wilt, there is no empty space for thee to confront.

Good is thy effort and well done are thy tasks, o worker. Make thy days and nights a busy part of thy realization and see the goals within thy sight become goals within thy touch.

Thou hast done well, beloved sister. Bow thy

head and seek the silence to know the size of my approval, the color of my reward bestowed upon thee, the warmth of my regards enclosing thee at this moment.

Chapter XVI

This is the story of the beginning of the world you know, the planet called Earth by you physical beings. It is in the belt of planets known to us as the Climactic Belt because the formation of your particular universe was of a more experimental nature than others of God's spaces and therefore was a sort of climax to his work.

In the beginning, Earth was composed of nothing living, just the metals and elements of its basic construction. Fire and water merged to form the mountains and valleys and seas of the planet. Before life was begun there was a long period— long by your time—of cooling and settling. The scientists of your physical plane have deduced these facts from the evidence they have uncovered, but they are mistaken in their theories concerning the beginnings of life.

The Lord caused the living things to be existent on Earth because that was his primary purpose in creating the planet—to make another abode for the creatures of his production in order for the experiment to continue in yet another phase.

Growth of living, breathing individuals was not a slow process, nor was it a process of evolution as deduced by science. Some of the human beings of your present world have evolved from lower orders of animate creatures, it is true, but also there are some of a high degree of development who were born into your world from other worlds, where they had been greatly-advanced beings working knowingly in the name of God. Still others come from neighboring planets also, not so advanced but having completed their tasks in their particular worlds.

The planet Earth is a meeting-place for many individuals on many different quests. Some are beginners in the journey to fulfillment. Some are developing well but still unknowing. Some are almost through with their earthly commitments and will be born into other worlds when next they embody. Still others are placed among you as leaders, as teachers of the truth which holds throughout the universe and all universes beyond.

Know each world abides by the laws of our

Lord or destroys its civilization time and time again, just as your civilizations have destroyed themselves again and again. Marterialism seeps into the weaker links of mankind and breaks the chain of love and progress holding all together.

Behind the seas of time lies true existence and beyond the hills of the future lies existence also. Earthly existence in the physical dimension is a matter of less than a moment by eternal standards, and by these do you exist though you are aware of them or not. They hold together all of the pattern for all of God's kingdoms.

High in the back of your consciousness lies awareness of your Lord. He is there whether you give him the courtesy of your attention or ignore him entirely. Always, at some point during your lifetime, you do become aware and turn to him for help. In the depths of misery you shall cry out to the Lord for comfort, in the clutches of danger you shall cry out for protection, in the traps of cupidity you shall cry out for deliverance. There are no atheists when all has been stripped from the material body and only the basic self remains. There is, at the last extreme of any trouble, no one to whom you may turn except him who should have been your first thought, him who should have been your constant companion.

When God created your world he provided for your protection in all manner of ways, physical as well as spiritual. He caused to exist nothing which could not be overcome by the strength of your faith, the active application of that current of God-power flowing strong in the body of the knowing.

Believe in the beauty of your world, though you see it not at times. When ugly things confront your physical eyes, turn your inner sight to the purity of the planet as the Lord created it, not as man has made it to be in his blindness and avarice. The core of all things is good and without malice or evil of any kind. Remind yourself of this when the ugly surfaces mar your view.

This is the mountain from which the clouds leap off into space, to soar aloft over the earth like balloons in flight. This is the mountain from which the rising sun can be worshipped in its truest and fullest extent. This is the mountain to which you may flee for comfort and safety when you become surrounded beyond your strength of the moment. This is the mountain on which you may rest your weariness in peace, on which you may worship in silence, on which you may give to God your most humble thanks in the knowledge your words will travel only a short distance to reach the spaces beyond.

This is the valley from which rises the scent of flowers to please your physical being and the mists of early morning to entice your soul to activity. This is the valley in which the shadows lie deep and quiet and sheltering for your fearful heart to seek. This is the valley in which to rest between mountains when your steps grow weary and you cannot climb further. This is the valley to which you may flee when pursued by the monsters of material living and the ogres of material thoughts.

This is the sea in which are buried the most ancient secrets of your planet. This is the sea into whose heart you may look for strength to carry your own heart high. This is the sea from which rise high fogs and heavy rains and storms such as the fearful cannot face. This is the sea in whose depths lives life, in whose darknesses you may see the wonders beyond your everyday awareness. This is the sea on whose surface you may adventure into God's great unknown, on whose soft bed you may sway to rest when you cannot rest elsewhere, on whose turmoiled tides you may feel the spray in your face and the joy of living to its fullest.

This is the earth where the warmth of birth begins and the cool of death writes finish to a physical living. This is the earth on whose surface you may see the growing of all that exists and the developing of all that seeks to grow. This is the earth from whose warm touch you may draw sustenance for your hunger. This is the earth on which you may spend the days of your life, and above which you may soar into the night-time of space. This is the earth which gives solidity to your existence, comfort to your fears of the unknown.

This is the sky in which you may lose yourself by contemplation of the stars by night or the blue depths by day. This is the sky from which comes rain to feed the thirsty earth and renew the roaring waters. This is the sky across which lightning flashes in the throes of battle between the elements. This is the sky which leads to other atmospheres, other planets, and beckons you with the irresistible finger of adventure. This is the sky which is a part of the endlessness of God's kingdom, the boundary of your atmosphere. This is the sky to which you may turn your eyes when you seek a physical symbol of the presence of God. This is the sky to which you may speak if you are looking for the Lord's ear into which you would pour your words of meaning.

All these and much more are the sum of your world, your creation. Beyond these lie many other parts for your participation, your enjoying, your knowing. Seek to know these and you will discover those lying beyond. Learn the near and you will soon discover you have reached the far. Believe in the beauty and goodness of the obvious and soon the subtle will have become a part of your knowledge.

Harken to the message of every part of your planet, for in every object you will find there is a message. You have only to listen, to look, to touch. Know the trees wish to tell you of their secrets, the rocks will divulge their knowledge, and the waters will whisper amazing things into a willing ear.

Awareness is yours for the seeking. It is as simple and as easy as that. Give your attention and you will receive that which you wish to find.

The heart of the Lord is in every part of his universe. So it is in the spaces of the great ones and so it is in the smallest leaf of your planet. He would share his heart with you in all ways, as you will share your heart with him when you find it is the path to true happiness.

Blessings are upon you of the Earth though you are not as knowing and as humble as you must surely become in time. The Lord shines his light upon you as it shines about those who work for him and him alone. Know this and be easy in your ways, for all things are good with him who says, The Lord is my shepherd.

Chapter XVII

Beauty comes in many ways. It is not always an obvious appeal to your senses. Sometimes it creeps upon you so subtly and so secretly you are not aware of it until it has entoiled you hopelessly in its golden meshes.

Have you ever looked deep into the eyes of a woman whose depths are beyond your knowing? Look, but pause not too long or you will have become lost, drowned in her enchantment and her ageless wisdom.

Seek the unselfconscious face of a child. Mirrored in its expressions is the beauty of all creation, innocent, clean and reverent.

Part the tangled growth around a still pool and see within the waters the placid mysteries of nature at its most serene and unfathomable state.

Beauty cannot be measured or described, for true beauty is as infinite as space, as varied as all the shades of the rainbow, as unmanageable as the delightful playing of fallen leaves in high winds. Let it wash over the shores of your awareness like the great experience it was meant to be for you. To encounter beauty is to have been privileged beyond counting, for it is the greatest blessing of God upon the sight, the senses and the heart.

Watch her walk in beauty who steps lightly as a wild deer, sinuously as a jungle cat, proudly as a pagan queen. Feast your eyes upon her dancing who goes as a moonbeam across the floor and is herself lost in the beauty of the music to which she sways.

In the eyes of her who looks at you with a thousand expressions and yet maintains the veil of mystery between you, fill yourself, slake your thirst for such are the eyes of the goddesses who roam the universe in pursuit of their godly duties. Beauty is theirs in all its phases, and the greatest of these is the atmosphere with which they surround themselves, the awareness so strong you cannot help but feel it though you recognize it not.

The obvious prettiness of pleasing features is a joy to behold, but for the exalted and religious feeling of gazing upon complete perfection look into the heart. A face may be irregular in form and still enchant the beholder. The most famous women of your world have been those of charm beyond description, magnetism beyond resistance.

Who could be called perfect of feature among them? Helen of Troy is an almost mystic figure of your legends, yet she was a living woman in her time. Her beauty has caused her to be legendary, but she was not classically perfect in her physical being. Great was her loveliness because she possessed that aura which sets apart the woman who is owner of it, which makes her strange but fascinating to a point of danger unto those men who can come near enough to feel its spell.

Nefertiti and Cleopatra of the Egyptians were not perfect in any physical manner, yet Nefertiti's beauty has been marked as the greatest in your recorded history and Cleopatra's fatal fascination has outlived the many benevolent deeds she performed for her people.

In your more recent times those women who become the famous courtesans of kings were wicked by your conventional standards but undeniably irresistible to even the highest-placed men. None possessed physical perfection.

Look to your present atmosphere. Pretty girls win first place in your beauty contests, not beautiful girls. The spark which ignites from within and consumes all resistance without does not hang dependent on the features or form. They are unimportant in the light of comparison with the magnetism for which there are no adequate words.

Make it your practice to look for beauty wherever you may travel, for if it is your great fortune to encounter true loveliness in your lifetime even once you will have an experience to cherish for the remainder of your days on earth.

Take the experience and hold it in your hands as you would hold a humming bird, carefully, tenderly, that you do not bruise it with your clumsiness or eagerness to retain possession of it. Beauty comes on gossamer wings and is easily marred by the crudity of wrong attitude or approach to it.

Alas, like the truly worthwhile in all matters of life, you cannot hope to keep it for your own for always. It must be given to many along a pathway and can be held captive by none because it is a rare jewel and is beyond price. Be grateful if you can know what beauty looks like, if you have experienced its touch and know its kiss. Be grateful and cherish its passing your way so you may become a better person for the knowledge of its existence.

Question not the mystery of an attraction when the reason lies beyond your comprehension. In the irresistible pull of her who only looks at you and enslaves is happiness of which dreams are made, fulfillment for which you dare long only in darkness of night, realization to which you can come by no other route.

Look into the eyes of the knowing and be sure these words are truth in all their most obvious and subtle meaning. Look into the eyes of the aware and be sure you will rejoice in your entrapment. Look into the eyes of the strange and be sure you have gone into the land of enchantment to which you cannot enter by any other key.

Beauty is the expression of God's great power at its most powerful. Beauty is the outpouring of the riptides of heaven and of comets across the sky. Beauty is the silent quiet of a look, the mischief of a sidelong glance, the promise of lash-shaded pools of laughter.

Beauty cannot be captured, it cannot be retained. Remember this and when it comes to you let beauty do with you as it will, for I promise you the richest rewards of all heaven shall be yours during its stay and the taste of its fruit shall remain in you until you become one with the spaces of eternal, everlasting beauty at its most complete and perfect state.

Chapter XVIII

The power of thought is so great it can encompass the universe in only a second of your time. It connects the minds of beings who are separated by physical miles and the hearts of beings who are existing in different planes. The mind is an instrument on which man may play as delicately or as strongly as he chooses, without fear of dire consequences so long as he persists in a good vein and not a destructive, a kindly mood and not a perverse, a loving attitude and not a hateful.

Whether you are separated from a loved one by the space of different planes, miles across the earth or only a wall between rooms, it matters not to your mind or his. In accord you can reach a telephonic connection which will act instantaneously to join you together once again. That your bodies are in separate parts of the world or universe means nothing to your being together in truth.

Death is like the caress of God on the tired brow of a human being. It should not be an event to anticipate with dread, nor should it be a sad bereavement. Liken it unto an absence during a short trip. Out of sight is your loved one, but vivid in your mind and heart, therefore easy to contact. Speak freely into the spaces beyond death and you shall be answered. There is nothing separating you from those you love except your conscious doubts and your need for self-confidence.

When a loved one is far away across your world, grieve not at the absence but let your mind fly to him as swiftly as the arrow from a bow finds its mark. You cannot feel a void between you who have communicated with your minds. The physical body is the one absent factor, and beyond any happiness it can know lies the realization found in sharing soulful emotions.

When one to whom you are tied in deepest bond is in another room from you, tear down the wall, dissolve it with the power of your thought-vibrations forging through. *You* are there, in that other room, and no barriers stand between you unless you choose they do so.

It is a hard lesson for the physical being to learn, that of accepting the absence of a material body without reaching the extreme of believing all is gone, lost beyond recalling. You must try again and again to accept this truth until you can believe it in all your trust. Then you will seek and find your beloved one wherever he may be.

Know the Lord has not made you know anyone so well and so deeply only to take him from you forever, or for even a little while. He is not a cruel one, your God, so it would not be possible that he should do this thing. He provided for necessary absences, journeys, adjustments, by making ever-constant the universal current. This it is which carries on it your thoughts in an instant so you may join any individual anywhere at any time. This it is which is never-weakening, always exact in its action. *You cannot lose anyone!* You cannot even lose yourself.

The closeness of mental contact between the spiritual and physical planes is beyond comparing to closeness of material relationships. Once you have learned to attain the one, you will not mourn again the loss of the other. Exalted shall you be beyond all parts of your present world in the sharing with your own of the richest of God's experiences.

There is never reason for giving way to despair, and the strongest of those faiths you need to carry you through material life is the belief you are never forsaken by the departure of another being, physically or spiritually. Give your trust to God in this too, for he leads you into happy living always if you but open yourself to his guidance.

Death cannot touch true love between two beings. It is as eternal as the skies about you or the soul which is you in any dimension. Serenity, sympathy and unspoken understanding lie between you at a distance as well as in closeness. Shut from your thoughts once and for always any fear of separation, oceanwide or worldswide.

Remember, love cannot be stopped by any barrier. It overcomes time, it traverses space, it ignores social taboos. Love is the sum of all living, the beginning of all great joy, the climax of all yearning. It cannot be bought with gold or with bribery of any sort. It cannot be forced or synthetically created. It cannot live in the heat of hate or grow in the weeds of prejudice. Love causes all great events and magnifies all little ones. It can end oppression of an entire country and inspire small people to mighty miracles.

There is no one remedy for any ill except love. It compensates for any material lack, replaces any missing experience. To him who has love is given everything, for love is the pure, undiluted light of God in full strength.

To defile love as it was intended by our Lord is to dirty the most beautiful phase of life. In its full realization, both physical and spiritual, love is an exalted state of being, a sacred joy. In the cheap substitution of bodily attraction only, he who submits to this temptation will lead his own step further and further from any possibility of finding the real love of his life.

Grant to all the right to love as he or she will. No one may say in honesty and truth that he is able to judge who shall be the most proper mate for whom. Only our Lord, whose workers carry out his wishes, can say with authority that this one is intended for that one. Station of birth or religious beliefs do not hold as a standard for all individuals, nor does age difference, or physical attributes, or any of the more obvious characteristics of human beings. So-called instinct is a sure guide to the one whose name is entered in your heart.

Hope always for the conscious understanding you will have need of in your dealings with others. This too is in the category of love, for you must indeed love him who would infringe on your time or help himself to your possessions with invitation from you. You must indeed have sympathy toward him who is constantly bemoaning his position or recounting all his ails. You must indeed feel compassion on him who is standing in your way to more desirable individuals or stumbles across your path through his clumsiness of step.

Behold the Lord in the love which shines upon you from the eyes of another. Feel the Lord in the love you bestow upon another. Know the Lord by the love in whose radiance you walk, in whose glow you speak and in whose blinding brilliance you live your days and nights, if you are true to your self and the awareness within that self.

Do not wait for love to come to you. Go forth and offer your love to all you encounter, in its proper proportion. Give the hand of friendship to the friendless, the word of kindness to the oppressed, the arm of assistance to the needy. Save your heart for the one whose presence in your atmosphere causes all things to change into their magical focus. But of other manners of love give freely. The fountain of affection never runs dry and the waters of kindliness are as endless as the sea.

Thy Lord enters thee when thou dost give selflessly of thy love. The Lord makes his light to shine more brightly in the darkness wherever thy love offers a small glow to the lost wanderer. The Lord has the word of his secret being to whisper in thine ear when thou hast ceased to confuse pity with love.

Cross the spaces to thy loved ones, mortal being, for thou art mortal only in thy visual self and to the God within thou art able to accomplish this too, as well as all other matters of the universe.

Give thy heart when the time is right that

thou shouldst do so, and in the giving thy return gift shall be of priceless value, for thou shalt receive the heart of another. In the exchange of hearts thou shalt realize our Lord until thy being aches with the exaltation and the ecstasy, and in thy knowing of his love shall his name be written forever in thy being.

Chapter XIX

Wherefore come the rains to nourish the thirsty earth, snows to cover the sleeping ground, ice to hide the foliage of spring and summer? All of these have their source in the mighty waters of the seas. From the seas rises moisture, to gather and bide its time until the heavens are ready to open and pour forth the accumulation of life-giving liquid to a waiting nature below.

Most essential of material elements is water, and therefore most powerful of material elements is the sea. From its depths come foods of all kinds, vegetation as well as flesh. There are goods like the fruits of land-trees and sweets like the sugar cane. All necessary chemicals with which to maintain the physical body are present in the living world of the deep.

Seek the water when you would build your strength to unconquerable proportions, when you would find sure calm and mighty power.

Look unto the waters for the sensations of God-knowledge, of existence beyond your usual scope. Flee to the water for medicine with which to bathe your wounded heart and sanctuary for your civilized mind.

Beneath the surfaces of the sea are great creatures and small, bird-like animals and elephant-like animals, man-like beings and monster-like beings, for in this separate physical atmosphere there lives a world parallel to your own, a world of shadows but of light-realization.

Those who have their being beneath the boundaries visible to your physical eyes live in the constant caress of mighty water. It nourishes them, it protects them and it gives to them of its powerful serenity. They do not worship at the feet of false gods such as material success and egotistical self-satisfaction. They have no need for wars with which to grasp the possessions of others. They are content in being, in sharing, in awareness.

The scavengers and marauders of the seas are not more ferocious than the wild beasts of your forest, nor more heartless than those human beings who prey upon their fellow men with avarice and hatred riding their backs. At least in the sea every creature is known for his true worth and his deeds are as public in their execution as any major event of your newspaper accounts. The killer is avoided because he is known for his black heart; he cannot pretend virtue until his intended victim is entirely off guard. The parasite is likewise known, as are the thief and the scavenger. How good it is that written upon each of the creatures of the deep is his name!

There are many lessons to be gained in a study of the known parts of your liquid continents. See below the peaceful existence when you look upon an underseas garden. Watch the obvious happiness of the small fish as they lazily sway with the movement of the water or dart about in their own games. Look at the plants, visibly contented, sweeping their tendrils with the rhythm of the sea.

Go beyond the shallows and seek the mysteries far from your dry shores. There are things beyond the common knowledge of present-day man, things to be rediscovered by the earnest, the patient and the daring.

Sea monsters are but large creatures which have lived for many centuries in the hidden fathoms of mid-ocean. At widely-spaced intervals one rises to the surface and is seen by your people. For the most part, they, like the dinosaurs of dry land, are uninterested in the taste of human meat. They attack only in fear of destruction by a supposed enemy and their wonder at sight of a ship is much greater than your wonder at sight of them, for their minds are slow and unable to encompass unknown things.

Beyond the mystery of the monsters is one which has not shown its light to your portion of the world for many centuries. Your legends speak of mermaids amd mermen, but like all tales they are treated by individuals with individual embellishments and omissions until the true origin is lost and only the kernel remains to haunt the mind with its possibilities even while it disdains all probability of fact.

To speak with complete freedom of all things of the water-world would be a waste of words. Some truths would be acceptable to the aware and the believing, but of all matters beyond human knowledge in the material world this is the greatest.

You may know this, however: The floor of the ocean is the dust of the earth. Water is like unto the air, containing oxygen, the breathing element for all creatures of the under-world. There are fish which parallel your birds, fish which parallel your jungle creatures, fish which are almost an exact replica of your domestic animals. Plant life is even more varied than your atmosphere knows, and minerals abound beyond the riches wrested from earth in your past knowledge.

With even this to offer as duplicate world, is it not a simple procedure for you to take the next step, to the point of human existence? Basic pattern there is to all of God's beings, in all of his universes. Should he then have deviated when he created the teeming life of the oceans? No, allowing for physical differences necessary to survival in particular conditions, all living beings respond to the same description. All possess a like spiritual body, a well-connected cord with all others. Though you know them not, or even of their existence be unaware, within your self lies that knowledge constantly.

Tides are deep and surging movements of the waters, and like the tides are the affairs of the depths. They may be likened to the breezes, high winds and storms of your atmosphere, and in their coming and going they pull with them the lives of all who depend upon them for sustenance. You too are dependent on the tides, and even your emotions are affected by their guidance. If you would study the tides you could have in your possession the knowledge of your strongest moments and your weakest, your finest moments and your most cruel, your greatest awareness and your most stubborn ignorance.

Walk along the shore when your worldly affairs will allow you the time for so doing. You discover new things on each occasion, and you build your faith in the power of the Lord, for in seeing the unending wonders of his waters you realize the endlessness of his ability and his activity.

When the heavens have opened to receive you once again at the termination of your present span of physical life, also shall the waters of the sea open to your knowledge and understanding, and you shall walk in the ways of the sea-beings and share their hearts with them. When you have reached the point beyond the zone of adjustment, the "River Styx," you will have entered the spaces where all things may become known to him who seeks with open and humble heart.

Take unto yourself the hope of heaven, for in the true heaven lies space beyond earth's atmosphere. There you will find no golden gates, nor angels playing upon harps, for true heaven is the state of existence each man makes for himself in his understanding of the Lord's intentions and his acceptance of the Lord's guidance. Behold the clouds and feel their feather-touch when you have cleared the hurdle between earth and the sky. Behold the crash of lightning across that sky and know the jolt of its touch when you have opened your body to the current of huge power such as no power-plant of your world has ever, or shall ever, harness.

Yours is the earth and all it holds, for the seeking in humility of all truth and the practice in complete faith of all God's laws. The sea itself shall open to you one day when your eyes are upon the dark pathway you must travel and they see only the light of God before you. Patience, mortal one, until that day. In the waiting despair lies lurking to grasp and devour the unwary, but to the strong and faithful the waiting shall be forgotten in that moment when the Lord embraces with his eternal flame the heart so true to him.

Chapter XX

This is the end of the story of the beginning, the sum of all basic knowledge, the final word of the universe as God hath created it. This is the final analysis in your primary study of your source, your inspiration, your accomplishment.

After each chapter in your life, pause you should to review and evaluate the lessons of wisdom offered to your consciousness. Pause and study, assimilate, put into active use each and every one of the profound drops of mighty oceans of knowledge.

This is the manner of your beginning and this is the manner of your ending, that you may now become practical in your application of all which has been offered for your applying, that you may become wise in the ways which have been opened for your feet to explore, that you may become fully as loving and faith-dependent on God as you have read that he offers unlimited love and understanding to you.

Close your book of primary learning in the ways of reaching the great light of realization. You are God and God is you. This is the basic truth underlying every word you have read, every meaning you have absorbed. Learn to seek the silence of space that you may yet know further the truths of the Lord's universe. Learn to accept with gratitude all matters of your material life, great and small. Learn to anticipate nothing explicit but only the happy anticipation of God's planned ways for you.

Be you humble before your fellow human beings because each is himself God, and yet stand you with dignity before all because you are a part of the great Lord also. Close your physical eyes to the attributes of your companion, the color of his skin, the shape of his features, and remember only that this is God within. Judge no man by his possessions, only by his heart. Greet no man according to his social station, only as he shall greet you as brother to his own self. Know no man by the words of his tongue, only by the truths from his eyes.

The Lord bless and keep you through all of

your days, as he surely will should you walk in his marked paths and do his designated deeds and spread his only doctrine.

Let not the words of others discourage you from your search for heights of eternal knowledge. To those who would speak loud and long of their own creeds turn an ear deaf to all except the tone of belief in their voices.

Only your inner awareness should be the guide for all of your days, the peaceful rest of your nights. Turn to God inside yourself, since it is infallible that he guide you rightly. The God within all others is present to the same degree, but since each man has his own being, like though it is to yours, let him confine his works to his own God-self. You are provided with that same light ray which cannot be misled or misconstrued.

Before the virtue of the truly humble man bow your head in honor of him, for he is courageous in your world of material standards, and he is lonely in your world of material relationships.

Seek the shadows alone and find the true God who recognizes no color above another, who considers no race superior to another, who withholds his love from none, who only gives in like amount to that which he receives.

Remember your fine self is truly with you always. What has been done in your physical errors is not so important as your understanding of the necessity for balancing those errors before further progress can be made. Allow your inner fire to burn brightly to light you along the way to your perfect existence in the material world. There is no darkness which cannot be dispelled by the light of God.

For long years you may have worked to accomplish, without success; but what were you attempting to accomplish? Are you happier for the trying? Would you be happier in the succeeding? Look into the reasons behind all of your movements, the motives of your actions. When they can be seen clearly and in shining cleanliness, then you may know they are of your proper pathway.

Always you shall know which way to turn if you will but wait for God's indication. Impatience is a mighty enemy to the material mind, but it can be conquered through hard effort, and the reward is worth all of the preliminary work. The Lord shows always the path intended by destiny for your walking. Choose it or not, you are the master of your own fate.

The Lord looks upon you with favor as you look upon his creatures with your love. The Lord touches you in approbation as you touch the hand of the humble. The Lord speaks to you with his finest blessings as you use only the tongue of kindness toward the helpless.

Sick shall be the mind and body of the ignorant until their awarenesses awaken to the light shining before them. Beset with worries and troubles of the material plane shall they be until they have cleared their conscious thoughts of the false gods and standards of your modern civilization.

Do not be among these, mortal one. It is written that none shall wallow in misery unless he choose to do so through ignorance or false pride. Give your being into the keeping of your heart, and let your physical self follow in subjection. All will be well with both if you will do this.

And now, we say goodbye to you until the

time has come for the next series of words upon the knowledge of the universe, to which you even now hold the key. Use it, and the treasures opened to you will be so magnificent your eyes will be blinded in their glow.

We wish to say thank you to the station for these lessons. She has served well and faithfully in all she has been instructed to do. There is no one so qualified above his fellows that he may say I am of the mighty ones, but we ourselves may say it for him.

No more shall we speak of this matter at present, but bear with you the knowing of the coming of one who sends forth the sound of heaven's own music, and the light of heaven's own illumination.

She wishes to withdraw from this of which we are speaking, for she has learned the lesson of humility through difficult days, but this we must speak of and she must listen:

Heart to heart we travel with her through her days and nights, and so close are we to touching that her material body is often overcome with the power of the current throbbing between us. There shall be no event of which she cannot be master, and there shall be no person who shall conquer her, for her name is Osmira and she is indeed beyond the need of the crutch of material religion.

We go now, secure in the happy knowledge that our words have not been lost as they have so many times before been thrown into the waste parts of space. Truth is never lost, perhaps hidden for a period, but never lost. So it is with all matters of God's kingdom.

Ijmubuti tan shima sin guki. Adj heraba thin gera shuj nati. Perha mu tis lashmoge fuiha, sin lahta, sin merahni, adj puchiko mer simohano.

The Lord is the name of all that is or has ever been or shall ever be. Treat thou all things in the manner of knowing this, that thy hands shall not be soiled by hatred, that thy lips shall not be festered by prejudice, that thy heart shall not be empty through malice. Thy God is thee, as surely as thou art alive in the world thou seest about thee.

For all of thy days on earth remember the loving regard in which thou art held for the mere reading of these words, and how much more shalt thou be honored in the Book of Days shouldst thou learn to understand them!

Walk thou in peace and love, brother and sister. Thy God walks with thee.

If you have enjoyed this book, we invite you to send for our catalog listing nearly 3,000 titles in the areas of metaphysics, religion, inspirational self-help, health and healing, occultism, mysticism, parapsychology and related subjects. The books are selected from the lists of nearly 300 publishers and suppliers, and are arranged in our catalog by author, title, and subject.

DeVorss & Company
P.O. Box 550
Marina del Rey, California 90294-0550